English Life in
Chaucer's Day

English Life
in
Chaucer's Day

Roger Hart

"God is deaf nowadays, and deigneth not to hear us,
And prayers have no power the Plague to stay.
Yet the wretches of this world take no heed of it,
Nor, for dread of death, withdraw them from pride,
Nor share their plenty with the poor.
But in gaiety, in gluttony they glut themselves with wealth,
And the more they win, wealth and riches,
And lord it over lands, the less they part with."

From *Piers Plowman* by William Langland.

WAYLAND PUBLISHERS · LONDON

G. P. PUTNAM'S SONS · NEW YORK

In this series

English Life in Tudor Times
English Life in the Seventeenth Century
English Life in the Eighteenth Century
English Life in the Nineteenth Century

Roger Hart

First published in 1973 by Wayland (Publishers) Ltd
101 Grays Inn Road, London WC1 and
G. P. Putnam's Sons, Inc.,
200 Madison Avenue, New York N.Y. 10016
Library of Congress Catalog Card Number: 72-84746

SBN (English edition): 85340 165 9
SBN (American edition): 399-11046-1

Printed in England by Page Bros
(Norwich) Ltd.,
Norwich

Contents

1 Chaucer's England: A Prologue

WE OWE to Geoffrey Chaucer in his *Canterbury Tales* a remarkable portrait of fourteenth century England. Although it is not, and in no way pretends to be, a work of history like the writings of chroniclers such as Jean Froissart and others of his time, it nevertheless is, as Professor Nevill Coghill has written, "the concise portrait of an entire nation, high and low, old and young, male and female, lay and clerical, learned and ignorant, rogue and righteous, land and sea, town and country, but without extremes." In the course of this book, we shall illustrate the people of Chaucer's time with extracts from the *Tales*, as well as from William Langland's *Piers Plowman*, the other contemporary masterpiece of English literature.

A type of hand-bell popular in fourteenth century England – Chaucer's England

Chaucer himself was born about the year 1340, in the middle of the long reign of Edward III (1327–77), who devoted much of his life to wars with France. Chaucer's family was closely connected with the wine trade: we know that his father, John Chaucer, was Deputy Butler to Edward III at Southampton in 1348, the year when the terrible bubonic plague, popularly known as the Black Death, reached England, killing upwards of a third of the entire population. Chaucer's mother, Agnes Compton, was niece of an official at the Mint, and with her husband she was able to bring Chaucer up in reasonable comfort – if not affluence – sending him for his early schooling to St. Paul's Almonry.

The young Geoffrey Chaucer then took the path traditionally followed by sons whose families had ambitions for them, by enrolling as a page in a noble household, in his case that of the Countess of Ulster, who later married the third son of Edward III, the Duke of Clarence. This training stood Chaucer in good stead, not only in official appointments as a mature adult, but also as a writer and poet, able to observe the higher levels of English society at first hand. His patron and protector was John of Gaunt, the great Duke of Lancaster.

At the age of about nineteen Chaucer went abroad to the European continent as a soldier, and saw for himself some of the campaigns of the Hundred Years' War, as the long struggle between England and France (1337–1453) was called. But very soon he was taken prisoner near

The fleur-de-lys on Edward III's surcoat shows England's pretensions to territory in France

Rheims and ransomed according to the custom of the day. Edward III himself paid part of the money towards his release, hoping no doubt for the help of a useful servant later on. Indeed, by 1367 Chaucer had outgrown the social status of his family and was serving as a courtier and about the same time took a wife, a lady-in-waiting to the Queen, called Philippa de Roet. King Edward began sending Chaucer on diplomatic missions abroad, as far as we know dealing mainly with commercial matters. For some time now Chaucer had been deepening his knowledge of literature, and had already begun to undertake his first writings which in the 1380s were to culminate in his life's masterpiece, the *Canterbury Tales*. By that time he had served in many more official appointments – he was a controller of customs in the Port of London in the 1370s, in 1385 a Justice of the Peace for the county of Kent, and in 1386 a Knight of the Shire with a seat in Parliament. He died in October, 1400, and was buried in Westminster Abbey in London. Fittingly for this genius of the English language, his tomb formed the first of the group that was to become famous as "Poets' Corner".

Country people

The communities and people of Chaucer's England were relatively immobile. Few ordinary folk journeyed much farther than the next market town, except perhaps once or twice in their lives to make a pilgrimage, or to flee from their servile status on the land. A rich lord needed to spend a good deal of money on organizing the transportation services needed both for his household and for himself. To give some idea of the slowness of communications, a good messenger rarely covered more than sixty miles in a day on horseback. If an entire household was on the move, fifteen to thirty miles a day was more usual, depending on the weather and the number of daylight hours at the time of year.

Medieval musicians depicted in a fourteenth century manuscript playing a cornet and a virginal

In Chaucer's day, farming in England was being carried on for profit, as well as for subsistence, as it had been from at least the thirteenth century. Many manors kept careful accounts of expenditures and receipts, compiled by the bailiff or steward (see Appendix on the Cost of Living). These accounts give us an interesting picture of the cost of medieval farming – the buildings, farm implements, and cost of hiring labourers by the week or by the day. The famous medieval writer on agriculture, Walter of Henley, estimated the costs of farming as follows: ploughing the land three times cost sixpence an acre; hoeing cost one penny an acre; reaping fivepence an acre; and carriage one penny an acre. Other expenses included for example the hiring of 200 sheep to "lie" on an estate for eight weeks to manure the soil; this cost eightpence a week. Marling (fertilizing) costs varied from three shillings and sixpence an acre to eight shillings. In 1331, the bailiff of Cuxham went to London to buy five new millstones. It was quite an expedition. It took him three days, and cost him five gallons of Bordeaux wine during the bargaining with the seller. When the millstones were brought back to Henley along the River Thames, the bailiff had to pay dues of wharfage, murage, and for the repairing of the river bank. As Chaucer pictured him:

And he could judge by watching drought and rain
The yield he might expect from seed and grain.
His master's sheep, his animals and hens,
Pigs, horses, dairies, stores and cattle-pens
Were wholly trusted to his government.
And he was under contract to present
The accounts, right from his master's earliest years.
No one had ever caught him in arrears.
No bailiff, serf or herdsman dared to kick,
He knew their dodges, knew their every trick;
Feared like the plague he was, by those beneath.

In return for their tenancies, farm workers paid their landlords in a variety of ways. Partly they would give their own labour services for a specified period each year, for example at harvest time; partly they would hand over some of their goods and produce in kind, and partly they might pay in coin. For example on one estate the peasants or *villeins* each held a "virgate" of land (12 to 15 acres) for which they had to plough, sow and till half an acre of the lord's land, and do various other services required by the lord's bailiff. They also had to deliver a quarter of seed wheat to him at Michaelmas, a peck of wheat, four bushels of oats and 3 hens on the 12th November, and at Christmas a cock, two hens and twopence worth of bread. They also had to pay the lord a penny each time they brewed ale. In addition, each of these villeins had to spend three days reaping the lord's harvest, though he received for this ale and a loaf of bread, and the largest sheaf of corn he could carry away from the harvest field on the end of his sickle. There were all kinds of variations on these themes, according to local customs and traditions, from one part of the countryside to another. Not all of Chaucer's Canterbury Pilgrims were described in such glowing terms as the honest plowman:

There was a Plowman with him there, his brother.
Many a load of dung one time or other
He must have carted through the morning dew.
He was an honest worker, good and true,
Living in peace and perfect charity,
And, as the gospel bade him, so did he,
Loving God best with all his heart and mind
And then his neighbour as himself, repined
At no misfortune, slacked for no content,
For steadily about his work he went
To thrash his corn, to dig or to manure
Or make a ditch . . .

Hardly any peasant dwellings survive from Chaucer's day into the present. This is not surprising, for peasant cottages were very roughly built. The materials used were those closest at hand – mud, wood, sometimes stone, with a roof thatched with straw, reeds or sedge. The floor was of beaten earth covered with straw or rushes, and the windows were small openings covered over with cloth or oiled canvas to let in a little gloomy light; the poor could not afford windows, and one can easily imagine how draughty these dwellings must have been.

Illustration from an early fourteenth century manuscript showing contemporary fashion among the relatively well-to-do

Edward II, a drawing dating from the second year of his reign (1308)

Most consisted simply of one room, which housed everyone and everything, including animals, around a fire in the middle of the floor – the fumes of which escaped as best they could through door and windows, since there were no chimneys.

One of the commonest types of peasant cottages, especially in the North, the Midlands and the West Country, was the cruck-house. This was built of a crude timber frame, the spaces between the uprights filled in with wattle and daub, or earth and mud, to a thickness of about six inches. The cost was very little to the occupant – the materials were found naturally, near at hand, and the construction was done by himself, his family and friends, among whom were probably the carpenter and thatcher found in many villages.

Few peasants can have afforded to buy any piece of furniture out of their meagre wages. Virtually all of their simple needs were satisfied by home-made items. The main object in a peasant cottage was a trestle table, which could be dismantled and stored against a wall when not in use. The only seating accommodation would be a few rough-hewn stools and perhaps a bench. Beds, where they existed at all, consisted of plain

Sowing, scattering grain by hand

Right Tumblers and jugglers were popular entertainers

Below Carting sheaves of harvested corn to the lord's barn

bags of straw or flock, sometimes resting on crude home-made wooden frames on the rush-covered floor. In Chaucer's lifetime, a jury assessed a prosperous villein's estate at little more than £5, of which £2 were household goods comprising bedding, pans, cresset, tripod, skillet and colanders for the kitchen, a cloth and five silver spoons.

The food and drink was equally simple and home-made. Most villeins breakfasted on a piece of coarse bread, usually made from rye, and home-brewed ale, made from barley. Dinner was usually a pottage made of peas and beans, with cheese and more bread. Supper might consist of eggs, oat-cake, bread, cheese and ale. Meat and poultry was beyond the means of most, except perhaps the tenant farmer who kept a few hens and perhaps a cow, although the villein might expect to have meat for dinner on the days each year when he rendered his labour service to his lord, for example at harvest time. As a contemporary put it, "Also in winter they suffer much hunger and woe. It would be a charity to help them. Bread and penny-ale are a luxury. . . . On Fridays and feasting-days a farthing's-worth of mussels or so many cockles were a feast for such folk."

These lines from William Langland's *Piers Plowman* show the struggle that the peasantry had to make ends meet in the Middle Ages:

> *"I have no penny" quoth Piers, "Pullets for to buy,*
> *Nor neither geese nor piglets but two green cheeses,*
> *A few curds and cream and an oaten cake*
> *And two loaves of beans and bran to bake for my little ones.*
> *And besides I say by my soul I have no salt bacon*
> *Nor no little eggs, by Christ, collops for to make;*
> *But I have parsley and leeks and many cabbages,*
> *And besides a cow and a calf and a cart mare*
> *To draw afield my dung the while the drought lasteth.*
> *And by this livelihood we must live till Lammas time*
> *And by that I hope to have harvest in my croft,*
> *And then may I prepare the dinner as I dearly like.*
>
> *"All the poor people those peascods fatten;*
> *Beans and baked apples they brought in their laps;*
> *Shalots and chervils and ripe cherries many,*
> *And proffered pears these present to please with hunger*
> *All hunger eat in haste and asked after more*
> *Then poor folk for fear fed hunger eagerly,*
> *With great leeks and peas to poison hunger me thought.*
> *By then it came near harvest new corn came to market;*
> *Then were folk glad and fed hunger with the best*
> *With good ale, as Glutton taught, and got hunger to sleep;*
> *And when wasters wouldn't work but wander about,*
> *Nor no beggar eat bread that beans within were,*
> *But two sorts of fine white or else of clean wheat,*
> *Nor no halfpenny ale in nowise drink,*
> *But of the best and the brownest that in town is to sell,*
> *Labourers that have no land to live on, only their hands*
> *Deigned not to dine each day on herbs no fresh gathered;*
> *Have no penny-ale given them nor no piece of bacon,*
> *But if it be fresh flesh or fish fried or baked,*
> *And that warm or hot to avoid chilling their bellies."*

The small tenant farmer, farming perhaps twenty acres, and freed of most of the arduous burden of labour services to his landlord, would have lived comfortably enough in Chaucer's day. A holding of twenty acres would have yielded an income of perhaps £4 a year. The largest charge would have been for bread, and a typical family consuming four quarters of bread a year would have to set aside a little more than £1 for this. Two quarters of malt for brewing would have cost seven or eight shillings, enough to provide about four gallons of ale a week. Meat would have cost another fifteen shillings to £1. A pair of boots would cost two shillings, and many of the clothes, such as russet

Musicians, like this harpist and violinist, often provided music during banquets and feasts

Richard II dining with some of his great nobles

Ploughing field strips with ox-drawn ploughs

Hunting and poaching small game was a popular means of supplementing food supplies among the poor

Lords and ladies listening to a musical entertainment

A fourteenth century artist mixing his colours

One of the few known portraits of Chaucer, painted when he was an old man

linen shirts, would have been made at home. On this basis, the small independent farmer would still have about £1 a year left over, which could be spent on building up his land holding – with land costing up to about ten shillings an acre, or providing for his daughter, or for educating a son destined for a humble position in the Church. Above all, this class of Englishman, which was later to be characterised as the "yeoman" class, enjoyed independence and a good degree of security of living:

> He paid his tithes in full when they were due
> On what he owned, and on his earnings too.
> He wore a tabard smock and rode a mare.

Men of poor origins could sometimes rise to positions of great affluence and influence in Chaucer's time. For example, Clement Paston, who was described as "a good plain husbandman" with about 100 acres, managed to borrow enough money to send his son William to school and later to train as a lawyer at the Inns of Court. By 1429 William had risen by hard work and ability to become a Judge of Common Pleas with a solid income, and by his death he left bullion worth £1,460 in London and £958 in Norwich, as well as manors and estates.

Workmen

It is hard to generalize about the standard of life of wage-earners in Chaucer's day, in other words those who did not make a living from the land. Some no doubt fared as well as the independent tenant farmer; others were extremely poor and insecure in their employment. Many wage earners were paid partly in kind, according to ancient custom; many received board and lodging from their master, plus a daily allowance of ale or cider, and perhaps candles or shoes.

An unskilled worker, whether on the land or in the towns, might expect to earn £2 to £3 a year, although he could often supplement this, for example by helping out at the busiest times of year in the farming calendar, especially the harvest, and haymaking. The predominance of industry, such as it was, in London and the South tended to keep labourers' wages at a considerably higher level than they were in the more remote areas of the West Country and the North. Apart from the men (and women) working on ploughing, tilling and sowing on the land, a landlord might also employ a shepherd, swineherd and dairymaid. All wage-earners on the land benefited from the after-effects of the Black Death, and the amount of employment which was suddenly made available. For example, a thatcher's assistant who only earned a penny a day before 1348 might earn twopence or threepence afterwards. But after about 1370 the increases tended to level off, although at a much higher level than had been known before.

It is likely that the wages of artisans and skilled workers varied more in Chaucer's time than they do today. A relatively unskilled artisan might only earn twopence or threepence a day, certainly before the Black Death had the effect of raising wage levels after 1348. But a master mason or master carpenter working on the building of a great castle or cathedral might earn anything from fourpence a day to ninepence or tenpence. Especially after the Black Death, employers tried to retain their best workers on a more or less permanent basis. A common arrangement was to employ a carpenter or a sawyer at perhaps two shillings a week, with the gift of a robe once a year. Exceptionally, they

Carpenters at work on a barn, under the direction of the master-craftsman

A housewife carding wool before it is spun into thread for weaving

A spinning wheel, on which the carded wool was made into thread

might be employed for life. An example of this was the contract between John of Evesham and the Dean and Chapter of Hereford Cathedral, whereby he received a guaranteed wage of three shillings a week, and a loaf of white bread a day. In addition, he had a "sickness benefit" of a shilling a week if he should fall ill for a long period – which in the Middle Ages was a common hazard. Although domestics were sometimes paid rather less than artisans, they were compensated by having more secure and regular work; most wage-earners, such as masons and carpenters,

Wrestling was a very popular sport, as was gambling on the outcome of the matches

If poor people had to travel, small children were usually carried in panniers slung across the parent's back

were only paid for each day they actually worked.

The working year was long and arduous. Even though the Catholic church calendar listed many holy days, these were often worked. A workman could if he wished observe many festivals a year, twenty or thirty for example, but he would not be paid for the days he stayed away from work. Working hours virtually took up all the daylight hours, ranging from eight in winter to twelve in summer. Work in the summer for most people began at around five o'clock in the morning, and ended at seven or eight o'clock at night, with half an hour for breakfast, and a rest of an hour or an hour and a half at midday.

Perhaps no period of history has left a greater legacy of building to its heirs than the Middle Ages. Over the roofs of every village with its mud huts rose the spire or steeple of a church; in every town there rose churches, and sometimes the larger outline of a cathedral or castle. There were probably a thousand monastic establishments alone, some of them very big, as well as several thousand parish churches. All these employed thousands of men: masons, bricklayers, carpenters, quarrymen, joiners, plasterers, sawyers and ropemakers. For example in 1377, when the population of London was about 35,000, no less than 400 masons were employed at Beaumaris Castle in Wales, as well as a thousand unskilled men. The building industry was probably the first to be organized on a capitalist basis, with the building materials and tools being provided for a wage-paid work force. The organization needed to sustain a large building programme was considerable – clerks of works, overseers, master masons, under-masons, and guardians of the lodges where the work force lived during the building programme.

The building of these great establishments cost many thousands of pounds over a period of years, and indeed generations. For example, more than £25,000 was spent on renovating the nave of Westminster Abbey between 1376 and 1532.

Apart from the initial building, the upkeep was a major task: roofing, painting, woodwork restoration, doors and windows. A private owner of a large property that needed extensive work might rent his own quarry for a period from a neighbouring landowner, and hire quarrymen and carters to bring the necessary building stone from it. These materials were not always expensive. For example, bricks cost about 18 pence a thousand, and even glass – once an enormous luxury – might only cost a few pence per foot. Rich men found it less worthwhile taking their windows with them when they moved. Two of the most expensive items in building were lead and carriage costs. Carriage, indeed, could amount to more than the cost of the goods moved. For example, in 1330 timber which cost 13 shillings to fell, cost another 55 shillings to cart off to Beaumaris Castle. The lack of roads – which so often amounted to no more than obscure rutted tracks – made carriage slow, and therefore costly. It could take the carters many long hours to negotiate potholes and flooded roads.

Wrestling "pick-a-back" style was a frequent variation on a popular sport

Merchants

In fourteenth century England the merchants were coming to play a greater part in national life, although commerce still occupied a tiny part of the population, most of whom lived and worked on the land. Chaucer himself was the son of a wine-merchant. The main work of the merchants was in the cloth trade, which was the foundation of many a family fortune, as we can tell from the splendid memorials still to be seen in parish churches up and down the country. Although they almost never equalled the nobility in wealth, many merchants were still able to support an affluent style of life. One fourteenth century merchant for example, William Haningtone, built a house with these lavish specifications: "A hall and a room with a chimney, and one larder between

Left A butcher cutting up joints of meat for the brine-tub on the left

Above A well-dressed merchant

the said hall and room; one solar [upper room] over the room and larder; also one oriole [recess] at one end of the hall beyond the high bench, and one step with an oriole from the ground to the door of the hall aforesaid . . . and two enclosures as cellars, opposite each other, beneath the hall, and one enclosure for a sewer with two pipes leading to the said sewer . . . and one stable." The very existence of plumbing in a house of this period testifies to the owner's wealth. In London there were many fine houses like this, on which the merchants spent the money gained from trading with their associates in the Low Countries and other European centres, or in money-lending and (often illegal) currency speculation. A merchant was one of the pilgrims on the road to Canterbury, as Chaucer tells us:

> There was a Merchant with a forking beard
> And motley dress; high on his horse he sat,
> Upon his head a Flemish beaver hat
> And on his feet daintily buckled boots.
> He told of his opinions and pursuits
> In solemn tones . . .

And accompanying him on the journey were others, perhaps less prosperous, but nevertheless jealous of their hardwon commercial privileges, protected by their guilds and livery companies:

> A Haberdasher, a Dyer, a Carpenter,
> A Weaver and a Carpet-maker were
> Among our ranks, all in the livery
> Of one impressive guild-fraternity.
> They were so trim and fresh their gear would pass
> For new. Their knives were not tricked out with brass,
> But wrought with purest silver, which avouches
> A like display on girdles and on pouches.
> Each seemed a worthy burgess, fit to grace
> A guild-hall with a seat upon the dais.

The market was an important feature of medieval life. Apart from the great international fairs and markets held from time to time in London and elsewhere, there were always the local shire markets held in the larger county towns, where people from the surrounding villages and hamlets could come, perhaps once a week, to sell their surplus produce for cash, which could be spent on shoes, finished cloth, pewter and other goods sold at the same market. One of the medieval words for merchant was "cheapman" or "chapman"; many medieval towns where markets were held had the word "Chipping" as part of their name, such as Chipping Sodbury, Chipping Norton and Chipping Campden. London had its own famous market thoroughfares of Cheapside and East-cheap. Once, markets had been held in churchyards, but a stop had been put to this in 1285.

At each market there was a place called the "toll booth" where disputes about prices and quality, and infringements of other local market regulations, could be heard and settled. In time, the toll booth became established in a corner of the town hall. The name still survives in Scotland, to signify a combined town hall and prison.

Affluent merchants and craftsmen, like the nobility, were expected to use their wealth for charitable purposes. William Langland suggested that the right use of a merchant's profits was to repair hospitals, help those in trouble, repair bad roads and mend broken bridges, enable poor girls to marry or to enter nunneries, feed the poor and prisoners, send boys to school or apprentice them to a trade, and endow religious orders. The Church, indeed, was almost as influential in commercial life as it was in rural life, and it was a rash merchant who defied or ignored the rules against usury, or the conventions of honesty and fair dealing which were relied upon in an age when the law was often lacking in sophistication in such matters.

Page from a prayer book showing two biblical stories, as well as ploughing and sowing

Sappho reading her poems to the elders; an allegorical painting,
it shows clothes worn by the upper classes

2 *The English Manor House*

IN CHAUCER'S DAY, life in the medieval manor house was lived by many on the grand scale. The disparity between the pittances of the villeins and the riches of the great territorial magnates, virtually untaxed, was colossal. Richard, Earl of Cornwall, brother of Henry III, had an annual income of about £5,000, and Earl Walter Marshall £3,350. The Earl and Countess of Leicester counted themselves amongst the poorest of the nobility, with revenues of around £1,000 a year. They were always in and out of debt, usually to the king or to moneylenders.

The country houses of the nobility were often fortified and moated, although this was becoming less common in Chaucer's time. Normally, the house consisted of several buildings grouped around a courtyard. Living rooms would occupy two sides of the square, and domestic offices the other two – bakehouses, laundry, brewhouse, slaughterhouse, spinning house, and chapel. The largest room in the house was the hall, which at Kenilworth House was 90 feet by 45 feet. Some country houses might even have two halls. Screens at one end of the hall led off to the kitchen, buttery, pantry and larder, and at the other end there was the lord's private chamber. Bedrooms were situated on the upper floor, along with small wardrobe chambers.

Yet even the greatest homes were simply and sparsely furnished. The greatest item in the manorial home was the bed, which with its carvings and rich curtain hangings often constituted the most expensive item among a lord's chattels. On the heavy wooden frame would lie a mattress, stuffed with feathers in most cases, covered in fine sheets, embroidered coverlets and pillows. The Countess of Leicester's bed was covered with a costly brocade quilt, and a coverlet of grey fur lined with scarlet. Apart from the bed, the only other furniture in the lord's private chamber would normally be a hard oak bench, and one or two carved oak chests for storing personal treasures such as his robes, armour, weapons, brooches and other jewellery. The most expensive piece of furniture known to exist in the Middle Ages was a great bed belonging to Edward III's wife, Queen Philippa, which was screened with green curtains, and which was valued at £203.

Travelling musicians, like this drummer and his boy, might be the only outside entertainment a village had

Board games, such as chess and chequers, were popular among the well-to-do

Transport for the lady of the manor, a satirical view from a mid-fourteenth century manuscript

The main features of the manorial hall were a raised dais, which stood at one end, with a trestle table and two large chairs or thrones for the lord and his lady. Below them, in the body of the hall, were similar tables equipped with long benches for the guests of low station and the household retainers. The hall was lit with great iron candlesticks. Candles were expensive, apparently because medieval cattle were so lean. The Duke of Clarence, son of Edward III, spent more than £60 a year on candles; a pound of candles cost four or five pence. The stone walls of the hall were often hung with thick tapestries of biblical or classical scenes, to add colour to what was otherwise a stark and functional chamber.

Food and drink

The manor house was, with the church, the focal point of rural life. Not only was it the residence of the great noble landlord; it was the office of administration of a large agricultural holding. All told, the

Right The lord of the manor at home

Opposite Winter, an illuminated page from a missal or prayer book, listing the holy offices for December

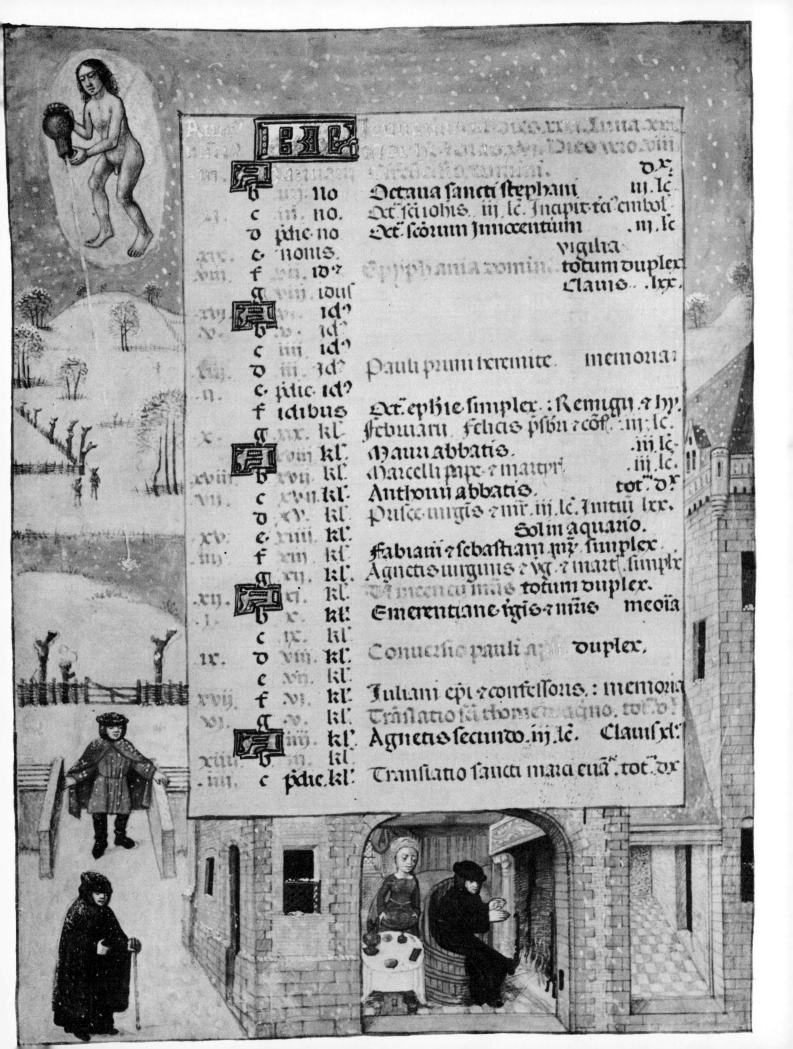

Octaua sancti stephani   iij. lc.
Oct. sci iohis. iij. lc. Incipit tra embol.
Oct. scorum Innocentium   .iij. lc
                                vigilia
Epyphania domini.   totum duplex
                              Claus. lxx.

Pauli primi heremite.   memoria

Oct. ephie simplex. : Remigij . z hy.
Februarij. Felicis psbri z cof. iij. lc.
Mauri abbatis.   iij. lc
Marcelli pape z martyr.   .iij. lc
Anthonij abbatis.   tot. dx
Prisce uirgis z mr. iij. lc. Initiu lxx.
                        Sol in aquario.
Fabiani z sebastiani mr. simplex
Agnetis uirginis z vg. z mart. simplex
Vincencij mris totum duplex.
Emerenciane igis z mris.   meoia

Conuersio pauli apli   duplex.

Iuliani epi z confessoris. : memoria
Translatio sci thome z ugno. tot. dx
Agnetis secundo. iij. lc.   Claus xl.

Translatio sancti maria euu. tot. dx

Blacksmith shoeing a horse in a wooden frame to stop it fidgeting

Two women carding and spinning wool

Horn player, a medieval manuscript illumination

house might form the meeting place of scores of helpers and officials undertaking a wide range of duties. The largest domestic task was to feed them all. The household of even a minor baron might include the following: a steward, a wardrober who was in effect the chief clerk, his deputy, a chaplain, an almoner, two friars with boy helpers, a chief buyer, a marshal, pantrymen and butlers, cooks, larderers and a saucer, a poulterer, ushers and chandlers, a potter, baker, brewer and one or two farriers, all with their own young helpers.

Shopping resembled a full-scale military operation. With the uncertainties of road travel, and of the fruits of farming, it was necessary to prepare for winter as if for a long siege: salted meat and fish, dozens if not hundreds of bushels of grain, eggs, apples, pears, wine and ale by the barrel, salt and spices such as pepper, cloves, mace, and cinnamon. The basic diet of meat and bread could be supplied from local resources, and the bread baked in the manorial bakehouse. But many items had to be foraged from farther afield, and many could only be obtained from London. The correspondence of many great houses is full of inquiries directed to friends and relations in London, Norwich, Bristol and other cities, asking the prices of various foodstuffs and other pro-

Swans were regarded as royal birds. Each year some were marked to show they belonged to the king

visions, and begging them to obtain a barrel of salted herrings, mackerel or cod, pots of treacle, eels and other delicacies. Pork seems to have been a popular meat, probably because it was the only one which could be eaten all the year round. Beef, mutton and veal had to be salted in the winter time. Poultry was eaten in large quantities in the manor houses – hens, capons, geese, partridge. Fish was also eaten a great deal, not only on holy days, but on most Wednesdays, Fridays and Saturdays all the year round. Eggs too were consumed at a great rate, in a big household thousands a week. Here is Chaucer's picture of a manciple, the official responsible for the catering in a large household or institution:

> *The Manciple came from the Inner Temple;*
> *All caterers might follow his example*
> *In buying victuals; he was never rash*
> *Whether he bought on credit or paid cash.*
> *He used to watch the market most precisely*
> *And got in first, and so he did quite nicely.*

Reapers at work harvesting corn. The bailiff or reeve stands behind to make sure they work well

23

The kitchen in a medieval nobleman's house, or that of a great monastery, was enormous, sometimes measuring thirty or forty feet across, and having a high roof through whose lantern (skylight) the fumes of cooking and the smoke could escape. The kitchen often stood apart from the rest of the house, connected to it by a covered way, in order to reduce the risk of kitchen fires setting the whole house ablaze. On one side of the great hall stood the buttery, where the butler (or bottler) superintended the wines. On the other side stood a pantry, used for storing bread, salt, cups and platters. The kitchen, preparing for a medieval feast, resembled a well-ordered and busy workshop. The cook's utensils included a *brandreth* (iron tripod) for supporting the cauldron over the fire, a dressing board and a dressing knife, a brass pot, a *posnet* (saucepan), frying pan, grid-iron, roasting spit, gobard, a *mier* for making breadcrumbs, a flesh hook, scummer, ladle, pot stick, a slice for turning meat in the frying pan, a pot hook, a mortar and pestle, pepper-quern, platter, and saucer for making sauce.

Illuminations from an Old Testament: on the right Ruth and Boaz in the harvest field; on the left an adulterous pair have been caught; the exposure of feet in medieval manuscripts indicated the breaking of the Seventh Commandment

Above Even in medieval times dogs were popular pets, as this contemporary conversation picture shows

Left Servants carrying dishes are led to the banqueting hall by a musician

Overleaf An allegorical painting showing men playing different kinds of medieval musical instruments

The kitchen had one or two open fire places. One of the kitchen's main tasks as winter approached was to boil the meat of the cattle slaughtered at that time, there being no root crops such as swedes on which they could be fed in the winter months. But joints and poultry killed for eating fresh were roasted on a spit turned by hand before the blazing fire. Bread, cakes, pies and pasties were baked in the ovens attached to the kitchen, whose thick brick walls retained the heat generated from the logs burning behind the oven's heavy iron door. The food and other items needed for a busy medieval kitchen were kept in the larder. One, for example, contained "the carcases of twenty oxen, and fifteen pigs, of herrings eight thousand, of *dograves* [sea fish] seven score, twenty pounds of almonds, thirty of rice, six barrels of lard, enough oatmeal to last till Easter, two quarters of salt."

What of the medieval menu? Chaucer spoke of *mortrewes*, of which the old recipe was for meat of hens and pork: "Hewe it small, and grounde it alle to dust." It was then mixed with breadcrumbs, egg yolks and pepper, and boiled up with ginger, sugar, salt and saffron. Fish pies were popular, too, for the strong medieval palate, served with sauces "poinant and sharpe". It is odd to remember that the medieval cook had to make do without any potatoes, which were not introduced until two hundred years later. Here is Chaucer's cook, who took time off from his kitchen duties to make the pilgrimage to Canterbury:

> They had a Cook with them who stood alone
> For boiling chicken with a marrow-bone,
> Sharp flavouring-powder and a spice of savour.
> He could distinguish London ale by flavour,
> And he could roast and seethe and broil and fry,
> Make good thick soup and bake a tasty pie.

Above A macabre game involving two men, one suspending a dead bird from his mouth, the other with a lighted candle

Above Servants laying a table before their lord's meal

Above Feeding chickens, the woman carries a distaff for spinning thread under her arm

27

But what a pity – so it seemed to me,
That he should have an ulcer on his knee.
As for blancmange, he made it with the best.

Spices were used extensively, partly to relieve the endless taste of salted food in winter, and partly to disguise the taste of vegetables and other produce which often arrived in the kitchen in a bad condition. The commonest spices were pepper at a shilling or two a pound, ginger and galingate at about the same price, zedoary at four shillings a pound, and saffron at more than ten shillings a pound. Cummin, anise, fennel, mace, cloves, horse-radish, nutmeg, coriander and "grains of paradise" were also used.

Cooks roasting meat at a tavern

Saving a swarm of bees. Honey provided by the bees was almost the only source of sweetness at this time

Beer was not known to Chaucer and his contemporaries: hops were not grown until the fifteenth century. But ale was drunk in large quantities, brewed from barley at about a halfpenny a gallon. Cider was traditionally drunk in the West Country, as it is today. Those who could afford it drank white wine, most of which came from Gascony, Poitou and Bordeaux. About two million gallons were imported each year in Chaucer's day – some of it by Chaucer's father – at a price of about £2 a tun.

Provision of food and drink on the grand scale permitted feasts and banquets of a kind seldom held since, and often the foods were served indiscriminately together. A great feast normally had a *pièce de resistance*, such as a boar's head, herons or peacocks, cooked and then replaced in their feathers and skins for serving. Knives and spoons were virtually the only form of cutlery known to medieval diners; but Piers Gaveston, the favourite for whom Edward II was killed, was said to have numbered among his treasures some silver forks "for eating pears". The

knives and spoons were often of beautiful design and workmanship. Drinking vessels, normally shared one between two, like the dinner platter, were rarely made of glass until the fifteenth century. Normally they were made of metal, horn or wood. The chief item of tableware, in fact the centre-piece of a medieval feasting table, was the great salt-cellar, often wrought of silver or other costly materials, and set before the main guest. Smaller salt-cellars were set before the other guests.

Another characteristic item of tableware in the Middle Ages was the *nef*. This was a jewelled model of a ship filled with spices to add flavour to the meal. Nearby would be the wassail bowl, or *mazer*, used for drinking toasts. Mazer is the old term for maplewood, from which the vessel was carved. Mazers usually had an ornamental lid, made of silver or some other precious metal. The dinner table was lit by torches or wax candles, by whose light the minstrels sang their songs, or recited ancient tales of courage and daring. Between times, the jester or fool employed in many great households would enliven the conversation with his

Above A knight out hawking

Above right Deer hunting, the chase

Right Snaring squirrels

Above "How to catch a woodcock", from a fourteenth century game book

Below Satirist's view of hunting and hawking

drollery. Sir Topaz, the subject of one of Chaucer's *Canterbury Tales*, held a feast before setting forth to fight his three-headed giant:

> "Go forth," he said, "my minstrels all,
> You story-tellers in my hall,
>   And tell me while I arm
> Romances such as may befall
> To Prince and Pope and Cardinal
>   And of a lover's charm."
>
> They fetched him first the sweetest wine,
> Then mead in mazers they combine
>   With lots of royal spice,
> And gingerbread, exceeding fine,
> And liquorice, and eglantyne,
>   And sugar, very nice.

Pages

Normally speaking, only the sons of the wealthy received much education in the Middle Ages. The son of a poor man, such as a small tenant farmer, however, could usually receive his education through the well-established avenue of church and monastic schools, and in most cases the only cost of this was the fine which his father had to pay to the lord to secure his son's release from work on the manor.

For the sons of the nobility, the best education was normally thought to be service as a page, and then squire, in a great household. Not only would the boy share a tutor to teach him reading and writing, but more important, he would learn all the social skills and graces needed by an accomplished nobleman. Often, the son's father had to pay for the privilege of entering his son as a page. One of the highest payments recorded was £1,000 for the four-year apprenticeship of a page to the Earl of Warwick in 1450. The boy fortunate to secure such a position would be sure of a good upbringing in manners, martial sports and social graces.

This extract from Hugh Russell's *Book of Nurture* tells a page how to wait on his master at table: "Put the salt on the right hand of your lord, on its left a trencher or two. On their left a knife, then white rolls, and beside a spoon folded in a napkin. Cover all up. At the other end set a salt and two trenchers. Cut your loaves equal, take a towel $2\frac{1}{2}$ yards long by its ends, fold up a handful from each end, and in the middle of the folds lay eight loaves or buns, bottom to bottom. Put a wrapper on the top, twist the ends of the towel together, smooth your wrapper, and open the end of it before your lord."

The page boys were instructed to serve their lord on bended knee, to bow when answering him, and not to sit until given permission. Grace was said both before and after meals. After the opening grace,

English hunt-servants in the fourteenth century

Left Slaughtering and hanging a pig

Below Catching herons with hawks

Above A game of club-ball

31

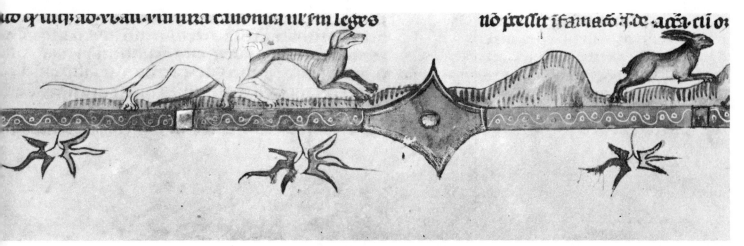

Above Greyhounds were used to hunt hares

Right Rabbits, which were introduced to England during the Middle Ages, were snared with the aid of ferrets

heralds sounded their trumpets as the signal for servants or pages to enter with their basins, ewers and napkins, for the guests to wash their hands before starting to eat from their wooden or pewter platters. Spoons and knives were quite common, although many people preferred to eat with their fingers. Good manners were highly esteemed in Chaucer's day, and the prioress in the Prologue of *The Canterbury Tales* – "Madame Eglantyne" – is a famous model of good manners at a fourteenth-century table:

> At meat her manners were well taught withal;
> No morsel from her lips did she let fall,
> Nor dipped her fingers in the sauce too deep;
> But she could carry a morsel up and keep
> The smallest drop from falling on her breast.
> For courtliness she had a special zest,
> And she would wipe her lips so clean
> That not a trace of grease was to be seen
> Upon the cup where she had drunk; to eat,
> She reached a hand sedately for her meat.

Academic education cost much less than that of a page. Indeed, the main cost for a boy at the University of Oxford or Cambridge was board and lodging, rather than tuition. The cost of remaining a student for a year was at least two or three pounds, although those with private means spent many times this sum on making themselves comfortable. Manuscript books were an expensive item, since mass-production of books was not to be introduced to England until a century later, by William Caxton. The cost of fine parchment writing paper was about ten shillings for 240 sheets, although imported paper was available more cheaply. Another incidental student expense was the fines frequently imposed for rowdy behaviour, a far greater problem for the authorities then than it is today. A list of fines at Oxford includes: "For threats of personal assault, twelve pence. . . . For drawing of weapons for violence, four shillings, for striking with stone or staff six shillings and eightpence" and so on. In the absence of town police, the university authorities had to undertake all their own law enforcement.

Hunting

The chief recreation of the medieval lord was hunting. This sport was an expensive business, even for a rich man, for it involved costly equipment and highly skilled hunting servants. The huntsman, for example, was paid $7\frac{1}{2}$ pence a day, and a fowler (attendant) almost as much. Horses could cost anything from £30 upward, and even a falcon could cost £5, and sometimes much more. King Richard II paid more than £21 for a pair of falcons which he presented to the King of Navarre. The hounds, too, cost a great deal in food and maintenance.

A typical baronial household kept a stable of thirty or forty horses, some of them splendidly equipped with ornamental saddles, bridles and cloths. The chief animal was the lord's own war-horse, which might cost £40 to £80 to buy. These beasts had to be enormously strong to carry the lord, weighed down in all his armour, and they were

Bringing a bird down with a hawk

a sought-after prize in battles and tournaments. The horses most commonly kept were the palfrey for gentry, the rouncey used by mounted soldiers in battle, and the sumpter-horse, or packhorse, used in baggage trains. When a household was on the move, one horse would carry the lord's bed, another his wardrobe, another his barrels of wine, and so forth. The Duke of Clarence had a "riding household" of 188 persons, with eight "coursers for his saddle", two palfreys, "a maile horse and a bottle horse . . . four sompters . . . seven chariotte horses" and two more horses to carry his litter.

Dress

The dress of a lord and his lady in fourteenth century England

In the Middle Ages, the sumptuary laws laid down in strict terms the appropriate forms of dress for each class of society. For example, a law of 1363 forbade the poor to wear any cloth except blanket and russet at a shilling a yard. However, since six or seven yards were needed to make a gown, the law can hardly have impinged on the lives of the poor. The rich on the other hand dressed themselves in costly silks imported from France, Italy and the exotic East. The materials in demand were baudekins (brocade), sendal (taffeta), damask and camulet. Very often the dress was trimmed with expensive fur, possibly on account of the draughty interiors of all medieval homes from manor houses to castles. Sumptuary laws laid down the fur appropriate to each social group – ermine for royalty, squirrel for the nobility, and deerskin, rabbit or sheepskin for ordinary folk.

Several writers of Chaucer's time criticized their contemporaries for dressing above their station. For example, the author of *The Regiment of Princes*, Thomas Hoccleve, wrote,

> *But this me thinketh an abusion,*
> *To see one walk in gowns of scarlet,*
> *Twelve yards wide, with pendant sleeves down*
> *On the ground and the rich fur theirin set.*
> *Amount to twenty pound or bet* [ter].
> *And if he for it have paid, he no good*
> *Hath left him wherewith for to buy a hood.*

The dress worn by merchants and tradesmen of the time

The beautiful simplicity of dress of the thirteenth century had, by Chaucer's day, gradually given way to noticeably richer and more extravagant fashions. The tunic, or *cotte*, of the earlier medieval period was evolving into a more close-fitting garment, like a coat, buttoned down the front, and generally hanging shorter down the leg. It was sometimes known as the "cotte hardie", perhaps since it was a garment strong enough to serve without a topcoat if the wearer was travelling or riding. The sleeves were often buttoned from the wrist to the elbow. The tunic-wearer usually wore a low-slung belt, which in the fourteenth century was frequently adorned and decorated. Those who could afford it had jewels sewn on, and carried an exquisitely worked dagger on one side. Over the shoulders, the *chaperon* – a form of short cloak – was still worn, though it was becoming more decorative too, being cut into long strips round the hem. A knight or nobleman would wear a hat made of felt, and sometimes set off with a rich jewel or brooch

A rich lady combing her hair

fastened to its crown or front. All the colours of this clothing were brighter than they had been a hundred years before.

The noblewoman's dress was evolving in a similar way. The bodice of her cotte was worn more closely-fitting; the skirt was fuller, and like the men she wore a richly-jewelled belt resting on her hips. Over her bodice and skirt she would wear a surcoat or *bliault*, with long-loose-flowing folds, and wide armpits, and often completed by a fur shoulder-length cape. One form of this cape was the *pelisse* which was fastened down the front with little buttons, hanging down in long folds so that it could easily be worn over the cotte and surcoat.

One could not buy readymade clothes in the Middle Ages. One had to buy a length of cloth or silk, and either have it made up by a tailor and seamstress, or – in the poorer families – by one of the women of the house. Three or four yards of black velvet might cost as much as a villein or smallholder earned in a whole year. Both men and women, among the nobility, wore jewellery, the women brooches, girdles and ornate head-dresses, the men collars and gilded cloths. Very expensive gowns were sometimes looked upon as investments that might appreciate in value, and which were bequeathed to favourite members of the family at death.

Gentlewomen wore their hair in jewelled plaits, often turned up at the side of their face. Some wore golden nets which completely covered their heads, while others, usually the older ones, wore the old coiffe and wimple of linen around their face and neck. Often, rich women wore a narrow jewelled circlet around their head.

Unlike the nobility, who dressed themselves with visits to the tailor and haberdasher, the peasant family dressed themselves in clothes made up at home by the efforts of the womenfolk. They bought raw wool by the sack, at prices varying from about £3 to £13 according to quality, and spun it into yarn for weaving home-made cloth. A few yards of this homespun made a gown or tunic that would have to do service for more than one generation of the family. Fortunate were those who, as part of their employment, received a yearly gift of a robe from their employer or lord. The guardian of the king's children received a robe worth more than £2 each Christmas, but those in lowlier employment received less, a pair of shoes or a pair of galoshes worth a few pence. In dress each man lived – and was usually compelled to live – according to his station.

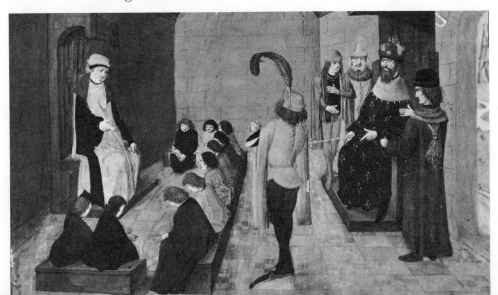

Left A schoolroom in the late fourteenth century

Opposite A courtier and lady

3 *Religious Life*

A MODERN CHURCHGOER would find many differences between a service in a modern parish church and one in Chaucer's day. True, the architecture might be the same: many churches dated back to Anglo-Saxon times, and some of the churches built in Chaucer's time had the beautiful Perpendicular style of Gothic architecture of the fourteenth century. But there would have been no seating for the congregation, except in a very few churches. Nor would the congregation have had prayer books as they would today. Indeed, most of each parson's flock were almost completely illiterate, and since the services were celebrated in Latin there was little for them to do but to join in the Creed and the Lord's Prayer. Not many parish churches could boast an organ. Those that did only had small instruments worked by a pair of hand bellows, although cathedrals usually had larger ones. Nor was there a pulpit; the parson preached from the chancel steps. Pulpits otherwise only existed for outdoor preaching – which was common – and preaching in the great cathedrals. On the other hand, churches in Chaucer's time had various features not usually seen today. There was, for example, the rood screen built of wood and sometimes stone, richly carved and painted, standing between the chancel and the nave. Above it hung a crucifix with figures of the Virgin Mary and St. John the Baptist on each side. Many parish church walls were gaily painted with scenes from the Bible, for example depicting the Last Supper, or – more eloquently – the torments of the damned. Few of these survive today. The walls were not the only brightly coloured feature: the priests' vestments were richly decorated, much more so than is common today; and the windows were brightly lit with stained glass. The Reformation had not yet come to England, and a Roman Catholic would find much in a fourteenth-century church to make him feel at home. Masses were said every day; some, at least, of the parish flock attended church more than just on the statutory Sunday. A modern visitor would have a poor opinion of the sermons. The priests were often poorly educated, even virtually illiterate, especially with the depopulation of the clergy after the ravages of Black Death, when bishops were hard pressed to

The seal of Oxford University, the main figure is a cleric, showing the importance of the Church in educational institutions

Opposite The assassination of Thomas à Becket, Archbishop of Canterbury (December, 1170)

Heresy was ruthlessly suppressed. The usual punishment for those convicted of the crime was burning at the stake

find priests of any calibre. A priest who had the means – and there were few – could have bought a manuscript book of sermons from which to preach. But there was one important difference between the clergy of Chaucer's time and the Episcopal clergy of today: priests did not marry. One of the priest's most important tasks was to administer baptisms, which were done more thoroughly than they are today, with the infant being entirely immersed in the water of the font. Many elaborately carved stone fonts still survive from the fourteenth century, and can be seen in little country churches in many places. The priest was also responsible for burying the dead. Marriages, too, were conducted differently, for church marriages were not regarded as essential.

A modern worshipper visiting a fourteenth century church would be appalled by the lack of good conduct during the services. Today, we sometimes hear complaints about women who go into church wearing shorts, and at men who are not wearing ties. But in Chaucer's day there were matters of more serious concern. The worst thing – referred to by many writers of the time – was the general bustle and commotion, even rowdiness. Perhaps the reason for this was not that fourteenth century Englishmen were less devout – in fact they were probably more so – but that the church was the only building in a village community where

Three more illustrations of characters from *The Canterbury Tales*: *above* The squire

Above The squire; a woodcut illustration from an early edition of Chaucer's *Canterbury Tales*

Above The shipman

Above A manuscript illumination showing a service of Mass in progress

Right The wife of Bath

Another of Chaucer's pilgrims: the pardoner

Above The Canterbury pilgrims enjoying a meal at an inn after a day's travel

Above Chaucer's miller entertained his fellow pilgrims by playing his bag-pipes

The summoner

all the local people ever met together. We find, too, that behaviour in the cathedrals was little better. In 1330 the Bishop of Exeter complained that during divine service certain clergy "fear not to exercise irreverently and damnably certain disorders, laughings, gigglings and other breaches of discipline." For example, "Those who stand at the upper stalls in the choir throw drippings from the candles upon the heads or the hair of such as stand on the lower stalls." Indeed, William of Wykeham, Bishop of Winchester, was even compelled to issue regulations against wrestling and slinging stones inside the chapel.

The "perfect, gentle knight" of Chaucer's story

The monk, another of the Canterbury pilgrims

Yet the churches of this time were usually crowded with worshippers, and were not short of funds to maintain their function. Some churches benefited from being a focal point for pilgrims, such as Becket's shrine at Canterbury. Indeed, so much money was collected from tourists visiting the tomb of King Edward II at Gloucester that it was possible to rebuild the choir, in what was one of the earliest examples of the Perpendicular style. The fourteenth century was not as great a century for cathedral building as the twelfth and thirteenth, but it did see substantial improvements at many places, for example Canterbury, Winchester, Ely, Hereford, Salisbury, Exeter, Norwich, Lincoln, Ripon, St. Albans, Wells, Westminster Abbey and York Minster.

Pilgrims

It was the lifelong dream of many people of Chaucer's time, as of earlier days, to undertake a pilgrimage – if not to distant Jerusalem, then at least to Canterbury or some other national shrine. Indeed, there were many such shrines. In 1313, Archbishop William de Grenefeld of York noted, "We have learned that a statue of the Blessed Virgin newly installed in the parish church at Foston is stirring up many simple souls as if something divine were more apparent in this statue than in others."

The pilgrim wore a special dress during his journey. It was the custom to let the beard grow, and to adorn the cap and gown with red crosses. One pilgrim explained that there were five characteristics of a pilgrim's dress. Apart from the red cross sewn onto the cap, there was another sewn onto a long grey robe, a long beard, a scrip or bag carried on the shoulder, in which the pilgrim carried his provisions, and if he was in the Holy Land he would ride on an ass. *Piers Plowman* described an encounter with a pilgrim:

Fourteenth century memorial brass to a knight

The cook in the band travelling to Canterbury

The friar

It was late and long when they lighted on a traveller
Apparelled like a pilgrim in pagan clothing.
He bore a staff bound with a broad fillet,
That like a winding weed wound about it.
At his belt he bore a bowl and wallet.
A hundred ampules hung at his hatband,
Signs from Sinai and shells from Galice [Compostela],
Many a cross on his cloak, and keys from Rome,
And the vernicle in front, that friends might find it,
And see by his signs what shrines he had been to.

Some pilgrims came in for his strongest censure for treating the journey as a kind of annual outing, when they should have known better:

A host of hermits with hocked staves
Went to Walsingham with their wenches behind them,
These great lubbers and long, who were loath to labour,
Clothed themselves in copes to be distinguished from others,
And robed themselves as hermits to roam at their leisure.
There I found friars of all the four orders,
Who preached to the people for the profit of their bellies,
And glossed the Gospel to their own good pleasure;
They coveted their copes and construed it to their liking.
Many master-brothers may clothe themselves to their fancy,
For their money, their merchandise they multiply together
Since charity has turned chapman [pedlar] *to shrive lords and ladies,*
Strange sights have been seen in a few short years.
Unless they and the Holy Church hold closer together
The worst misery of man will mount up quickly.

According to Chaucer, pilgrims spent a good deal of their time on the journey singing and carousing. The Miller, for example, took along

The canon's yeoman

The clerk of Oxford

45

Caught! A monk and his ladyfriend in the stocks, a satirist's view of laxity in the Church

The franklin

his bagpipes, for "a bagpipe well could he blow and sounden, and therewithal he brought us out of town"; while the Pardoner and the Summoner used to pass the time by singing duets. Not all pilgrims, of course, were so light-hearted. For them, the pilgrimage was the greatest act of devotion they made in their lives. Some even branded themselves with the cross, or cut themselves: "With a sharp knife he share [sheared] a cross upon his shoulder bare."

The greatest place of pilgrimage in England was, of course, Canterbury – the subject of *The Canterbury Tales,* and the shrine of St. Thomas-à-Becket, slain by four knights on 29th December, 1170, after his quarrel with King Henry II. The second centenary of the event took place in Chaucer's lifetime, and for this jubilee thousands of people took to the road, and there was free food and drink laid on all the way from London on the road south. Bishop Simon Sudbury of London overtook a band of cheerful merrymakers on the road, and exclaimed, "Plenary indulgences for your sins by repairing to Canterbury? Better hope might ye have of Salvation had ye stayed at home and brought forth fruits meet for repentance!" But a Kentish squire called Thomas of Aldon angrily retorted, "My Lord Bishop, for that you have thus spoken evil of St. Thomas and are minded to stir up the minds of the people against him, I will give up mine own salvation if you yourself do not die a most shameful death!" Eleven years later, Sudbury, then Archbishop of Canterbury, was slain on Tower Hill.

The nun's priest (*left*) and the prioress were also members of the band travelling to Becket's shrine in Canterbury

Superstition surrounded the whole business of Canterbury. If the body of St. Thomas were not enough to satisfy the curious pilgrims, there were other relics: the whole arms of eleven saints, the bed of the Blessed Virgin, some wool of her own weaving, a fragment of the rock at Calvary, a piece of rock from the Holy Sepulchre, Aaron's rod, a piece of the clay from which Adam was made, and other spectacular exhibits. Nothing, it seemed, was too much for the credulity of the sensation-seeking tourists.

Monks, friars and priests

Apart from the Churches, there was another side to English religious life, a side which as a result of the Reformation of Henry VIII has almost completely disappeared. This was the religious life of the monks and friars. At this time, almost every large building on the English landscape which was not a castle or manor house was almost certain to be a religious house of some kind. Many of these were monasteries and nunneries. Their traditions ran back to the time of the early Christian Church, when bands of devout Christians wished to retire from secular life and dedicate their lives entirely to prayer and the service of God and man. The religious foundations were governed by rules of poverty, obedience, chastity and self-mortification laid down by St. Benedict. The best known religious orders were those of the Cluniacs or Benedictines, who wore black robes; the Cistercians who

A slightly irreverent view of a parish clerk sprinkling a knight and his lady with holy water

wore white robes; and the Carthusians, who also wore white, and shaved the whole of their heads. The Carthusians were the strictest of the three; they hardly spoke at all, and ate only one meal a day.

The friars – from the French *frère* meaning brother – took a different view. Following the life of St. Francis of Assisi and St. Dominic, they devoted themselves, not to withdrawing from the world like the monks, but to going about and preaching the Gospel. Living entirely upon charity, at least in theory, these friars journeyed about the countryside, visiting the towns and parishes. But by Chaucer's time the friars were beginning to fall into disrepute, with much of their original idealism evaporated, and their style of living more comfortable. The friars were a common sight in Chaucer's England, and formed a major part of the large religious community. Of the thirty pilgrims who set forth from the Tabard Inn in London in April 1387, the Canterbury Pilgrims of Chaucer's imagination, no less than eleven were clerics; and the Canon who joined the company near Canterbury made twelve. Chaucer clearly did not have a high opinion of his own characters, and indeed there is much else in contemporary literature to show that they were entirely believable human beings. Chaucer was particularly scathing about the Monk:

> This Monk was therefore a good man to horse;
> Greyhounds he had, as swift as birds, to course.
> Hunting a hare or riding at a fence
> Was all his fun, he spared for no expense.

I saw his sleeves were garnished at the hand
With fine grey fur, the finest in the land,
And on his hood, to fasten it at his chin
He had a wrought-gold cunningly fashioned pin;
Into a lover's knot it seemed to pass.
His head was bald and shone like looking-glass;
So did his face, as if it had been greased.
He was a fat personable priest;
His prominent eyeballs never seemed to settle.
They glittered like the flames beneath a kettle;
Supple his boots, his horse in fine condition.
He was a prelate fit for exhibition,
He was not pale like a tormented soul.
He liked a fat swan best, and roasted whole.

The general confusion characteristic of most medieval battles

Nor did Chaucer have much time for the Pardoner, who made his living by selling indulgences – papers issued by the Pope, often forged, which purported to reduce the time spent in purgatory by the buyer after his death. A big sin called for an expensive indulgence:

> *His wallet lay before him on his lap,*
> *Brimful of pardons come from Rome all hot.*

The Pardoner was certainly talented at his job:

> *How well he read a lesson or told a story!*
> *But best of all he sang an Offertory,*
> *For well he knew that when that song was sung*
> *He'd have to preach and tune his honey-tongue*
> *And (well he could) win silver from the crowd.*
> *That's why he sang so merrily and loud.*

But *Piers Plowman* sounded a dire note of warning to those who set too much store by such hopes:

> *You who purchase your pardons and papal quarters,*
> *At the dread doom, when the dead shall rise,*
> *And all come before Christ, and give full accounting,*
> *When the doom will decide what day by day you practised,*
> *How you led your life and were lawful before him,*
> *Though you have pocketfuls of pardons there, or provincial letters,*
> *Though you be found in the fraternity of all the four orders,*
> *Though you have double indulgences – Unless Do Well help you*
> *I set not your patents and your pardons at the worth of a peascod!*

Of all the clerics in the *Canterbury Tales* it is the humble country parson who comes out best. Despite his poverty and lowly station, so far below that of the fur-clad bishop to whom he was responsible, he deserved praise:

> *Wide was his parish, with houses far asunder,*
> *Yet he neglected not in rain or thunder,*
> *In sickness or in grief, to pay a call*
> *On the remotest, whether great or small.*

We have some idea of the quality of the clergy from the bishops' reports which were compiled from time to time in the dioceses, although to be fair these naturally concentrated attention on what was wrong rather than what was right. One complaint, heard at intervals, was about nuns who went on pilgrimages, which they were not supposed to do – since pilgrimages had begun to resemble an annual outing in many respects rather than a real act of devotion and sacrifice. Monks were more and more condemned for spending their time on hunting and good food rather than on their devotions. Indeed, by Chaucer's time monks were commonly paid a wage for their duties, which ran directly against the spirit of poverty laid down by the rule of St. Benedict. The Prioress in the *Canterbury Tales* was noted for her dogs, and this again would have earned the reproof of many a bishop. In 1387, the very year when the Canterbury Pilgrims, including the Prioress, set off from London, Bishop William of Wykeham was reprimanding the Abbess of Romsey in Hampshire on exactly this question of keeping pets.

By Chaucer's time, another important change had taken place in the status of the monasteries. No longer were they the sole repositories of learning. Once, monasteries had been the only places where the old manuscripts were copied out by hand for the use of scholars. But Chaucer, as a layman, was engaged on similar work at Court, in what was really a civil service capacity. And in any case, the Universities of Oxford and Cambridge had by now assumed the highest place in scholarship. Houses were established at each for monks who wished to study there, but the monks had to be clever to secure a place which was no longer theirs by right and tradition.

Those who complained about the moral laxity and general decline of the old standards of the monks could now turn, if they wished, to the Lollards, as the followers of John Wycliffe were known. More active after his death in 1384 than before, they played an important part in drawing attention to the worldliness and insincerity of the Church, and in their travels about the countryside sometimes brought with them parts of Wycliffe's new translation of the Bible into English. And for the first time, ordinary English men and women could hear the Lord's Prayer recited in their native tongue: "Dure fadir that art in hevenes, halewid be thi name; thi kyngdoom come to, be thi wille done in arthe as in hevene; gyve to us this dai oure breed . . . And forgyve to us oure dettis, as we forgyven to oure dettouries; and lede us not into temptacioun, but delyvere us fro yvel. Amen."

Wycliffe and his followers attracted bitter opposition from many members of the Church for their new ideas. As a contemporary chronicler explained, "Among other unspeakable things he denied that the Pope is able to excommunicate anyone . . . and said moreover that neither the King nor any secular lord could give property in perpetuity to any person or church." Wycliffe, indeed, proposed that the Church should give up all its temporal possessions and concentrate on the business of saving souls. Much of the reason for the bitterness of the attacks on Wycliffe stemmed from the fact that his followers, exaggerating some of his ideas, denounced all landowners, not only the Church. As a satirist put it,

> *All stipends they forbid to give*
> *And tithes whereon poor curates live.*
> *From sinful lords their dues they take,*
> *Bid serfs their services forsake.*

These were certainly revolutionary ideas, and as we shall see in a later chapter, were to contribute to the unrest which reached its climax in the shape of the Peasants' Revolt in 1381.

4 *War and Chivalry*

THE MID FOURTEENTH CENTURY saw the start of the long episodic hostilities between England and France known as the Hundred Years' War (1338–1453), which contained the great English victory of Crécy in 1346, which took place when Chaucer was a boy. This period saw the old supremacy of the mounted knight in decline: English infantrymen were beginning to establish the power of the longbow; the immensely long pike of the Swiss was used to deadly effect; and at Crécy cannon were used, admittedly to little advantage at this early date.

Two kings conferring before battle

Fighting men

There was a strict scale of daily pay for the fighting men, from the highest rank to the lowest. It ranged from twenty shillings a day for the young Prince of Wales, six shillings and eightpence for earls, four shillings for barons, two shillings for knights, threepence for the archers and twopence for the Welsh spearmen, who were incidentally each provided with a cloak and tunic by the government. The archers wore iron caps, and apart from their bow of more than six feet long they carried a sword and dagger. The arrows, which measured three feet, were made of wood, and tipped with a barbed iron point to make them difficult to extract from their human targets. Their shafts were winged with feathers of goose or peacock. The range was considerable, about 240 yards, and skilled archers could fire as many as twelve arrows a minute, a good deal faster than the older weapon of the crossbow still preferred by many of England's continental adversaries. The English army was accompanied at Crécy by a small band of musicians including five trumpeters, a drummer, and wind and string instrumentalists, though among the Scots each man carried his own horn, blowing together "to frighten their enemies and cheer themselves."

Military service was closely linked with the feudal system, with its characteristic bond between master and man. Once upon a time, military service had been part of every tenant's obligation to his lord, but by Edward III's time money payments such as scutage (shield

money) had become the more normal practice. The greatest lords had
indentures with the King which set out in some detail the terms of their
military service – for example not only pay, but compensation for the
loss of horses in battle, rights over prisoners held for ransom, and other
matters. Many tenants, at all levels of society, had commuted their
old feudal-style military obligations with cash payments, which in
turn allowed the King to hire his troops and commanders at the daily
rate.

Sometimes, an indenture provided for a knight or nobleman to
bring other soldiers to serve with him. For instance, this indenture
sealed at Pontefract in 1381 between John of Gaunt (Duke of Lancaster)
and one William Tunstall stipulated that in time of war William should
receive "by the hands of the Duke's treasurer of war, such wages and

A heavily armoured knight was very vulnerable once he had been
unseated from his horse

Siege warfare was common. Thick walls, drawbridges and slit windows, were powerful defences against the attackers

Men-at-arms, such as these two, usually fought on foot during battle

A knight bidding farewell to his lady before leaving for the war

consideration for himself and the men-at-arms and archers, which he shall bring at the Duke's command, as the Duke himself receives from the King of England for men-at-arms and archers of similar condition. Or, if the Duke is campaigning on his own, as much as he gives to other esquires, men-at-arms, and archers."

For some men, especially the "men-at-arms" – the knights and squires who aspired to become knights – warfare was not merely a duty, it was an opportunity for social advancement, for success in battle could be amply rewarded by a grateful commander. Mostly, these men fought on foot, although they brought three or four horses each on their campaigns, a stallion and one or two geldings or mares. Their baggage also included many items of personal comfort and pleasure. One knight took with him a large pack of hounds. Sometimes the knights took to horseback to mount a charge, as they did at the great battle of Poitiers in 1356 when the commander, the Black Prince, ordered a charge to rally his forces.

By the mid-fourteenth century a typical feature of the army were the *hobelars* or light horsemen, whose armour generally consisted of a haketon, a bascinet (head-piece), a vizor (face-guard), and iron

Two knights tilting at each other during a joust

Opposite Illuminated page from a fourteenth century treatise on medical matters

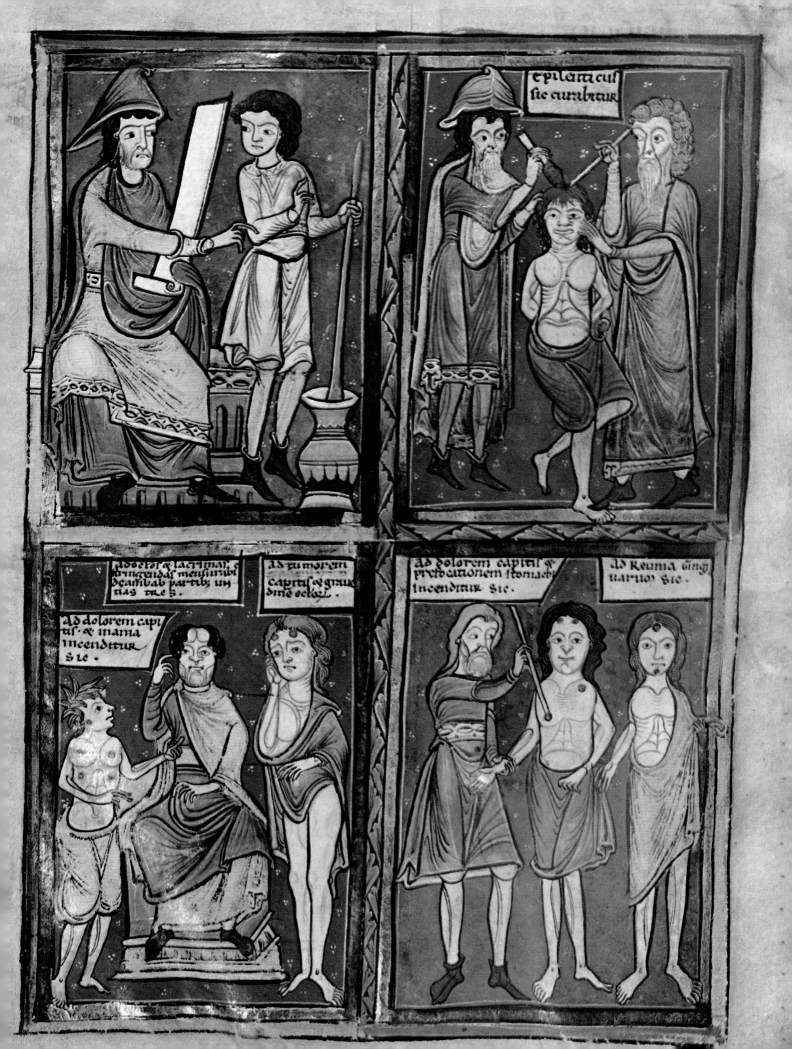

epileticuſ
ſic curabitur

ad tumorem
capitis & grauit-
dine oculi.

ſadoctos & lacrimaſ, &
ſtringendaſ menſuribi
dcaſiabab partibuſ uſ
tiaſ rreſ.

ad dolorem capi
tiſ & manıa
incenditur
ſic.

ad dolorem capitiſ &
preſdicationem ſtomaci
incenditur ſic.

ad Reunia ơingi
uarrưở ſic.

Above The clerk, one of Chaucer's pilgrims, holding his beads on his way to Becket's shrine at Canterbury

Below The nun. Pilgrimages to the shrines of saints were part of her duty

Above The wife of Bath: pilgrims like her, who regarded their pilgrimages more as a holiday outing were much criticized by the Church

Below Even on pilgrimage the knight wore his sword and spurs. In the background his shield hangs in a tree, an allusion to the custom adopted by knights before taking part in a tournament

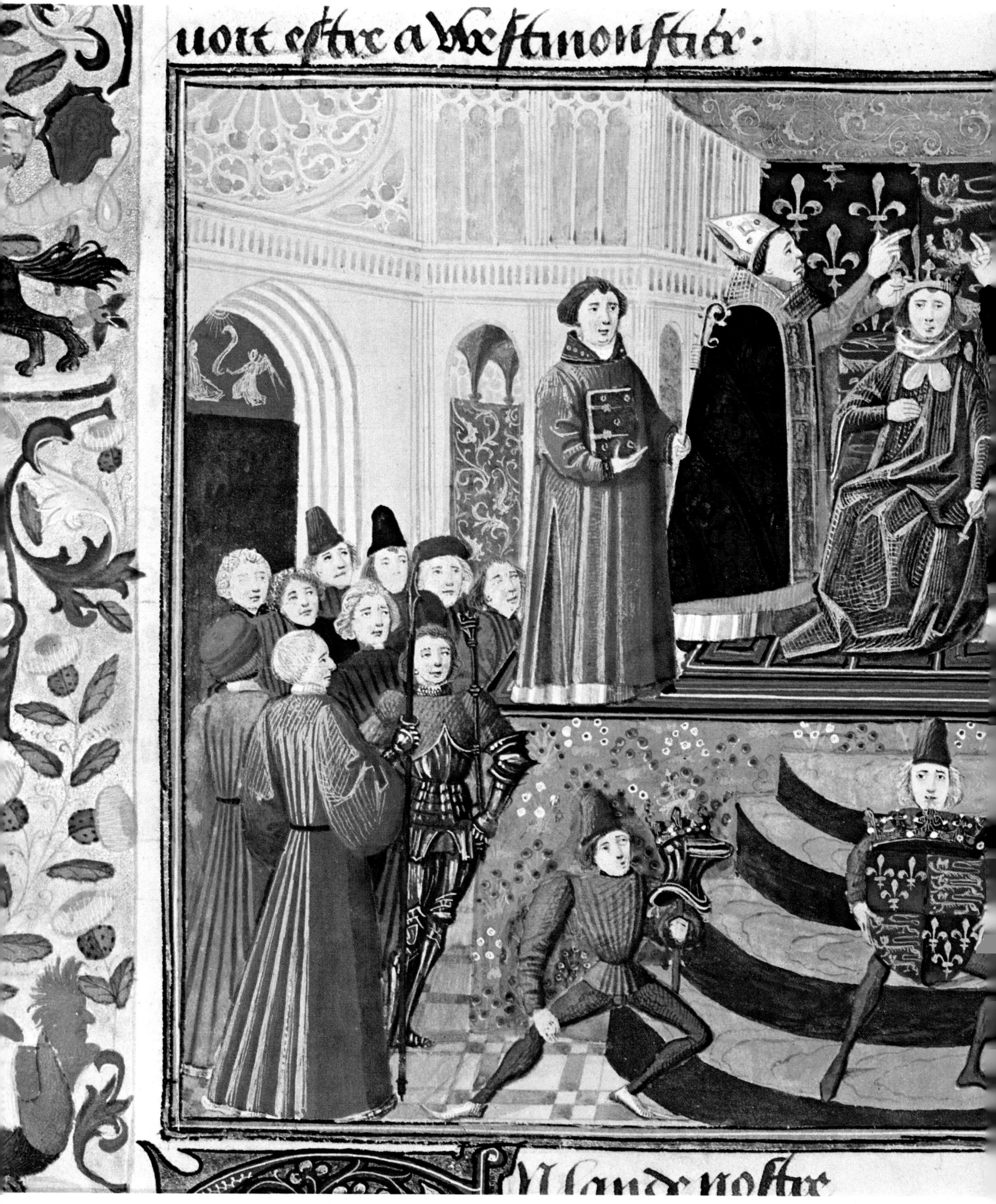
uoit estre a Westmonstier.
lande nostre

terre la qluet mut partie. Et

The coronation of Henry IV, 1399. The archbishops of York and Canterbury bless the king after the crown has been placed on his head. On the steps of the throne pages bear the king's crowned helm, his coat-of-arms and sword

Whan for his seynt god werkith bi myracle

Quarta subit mortem prosternit
tercia sortem. februarius.

Opposite above Masons hard at work building a church under the direction of the master-mason, while the king looks on

Opposite below A man warms himself by the fire. Note the glazed window, stone fire-place and bed with hangings and linen sheets, all these indicate the home of a wealthy man

Top The Peasants' Revolt: two groups of rebels, one led by Wat Tyler *left* the other by John Ball, meet outside London

Left The funeral procession of Richard II, 1399. The new king, Henry IV, made sure Richard had an elaborate funeral in London to allay the rumours circulating about the circumstances of the former king's death

Craftsmen at work: *top* tailors embroider a cloak for a rich
merchant and *below* skilled craftsmen work on a carved ornament
for a church

gauntlets. For arms they carried a sword, knife and lance. Their wage was sixpence a day.

Nowadays, all knighthoods are conferred by the Queen in person. But in the fourteenth century it often happened that a squire who had done well in battle was knighted in the hour of victory by the commanding general. The knight then became entitled to wear gilded spurs – hence the phrase "to win one's spurs". Geoffrey Chaucer himself served

Military devices used in siege warfare to break the besieged castle's defences

Two armies about to meet in battle before a besieged fortress

Overleaf Beaumaris Castle in Wales was built by Edward I as a stronghold of English rule against the Welsh

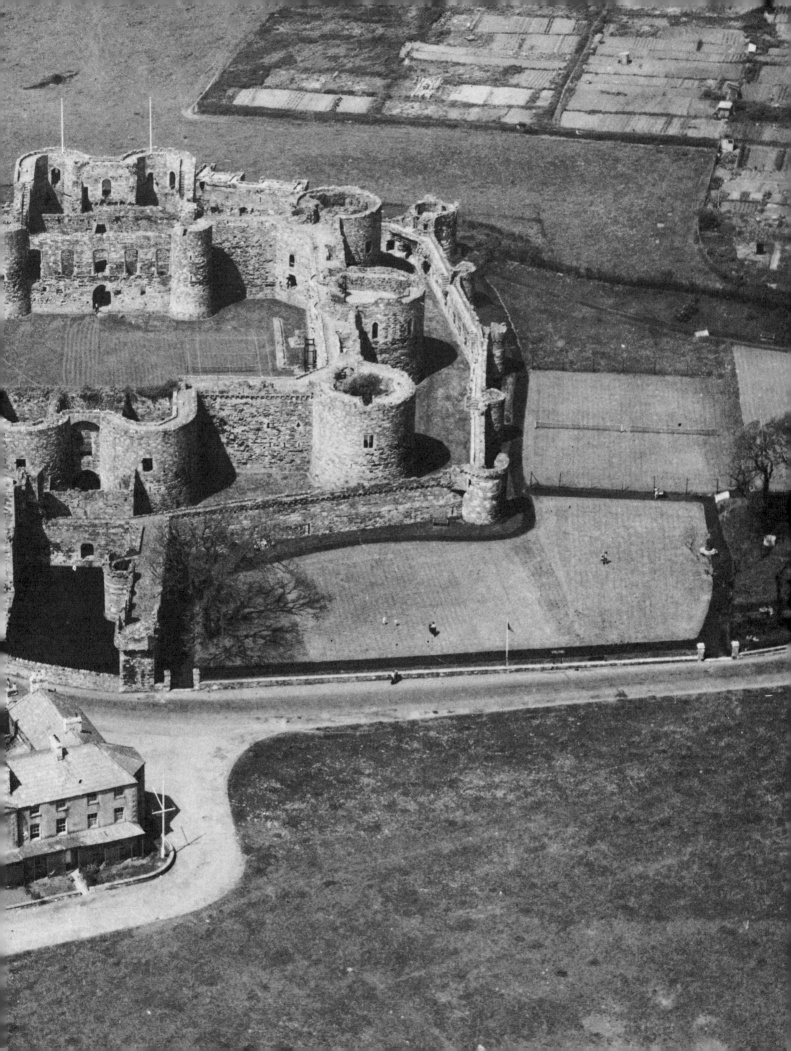

Crusaders arriving by sea to attack a citadel held by the Saracens

The attacking force encamped around the besieged city

as a page, and became a squire, but he never achieved knighthood. A high code of conduct was expected from a knight, and this code of chivalry was at its height in Chaucer's day. Sometimes it was carried to extremes: for example, after taking the French king prisoner at the Battle of Poitiers, the Black Prince waited on him at table himself, and on returning home to London he allowed his royal charge to ride before him on a fine white stallion. The literature of the period is filled with heroic romances of the semi-legendary King Arthur and other figures famous for their chivalrous exploits. Some knights spent their whole lives seeking adventures in battle, not just for their own country and king, but as roving "free lances". Colourful blazons and crests were an important part of the pageantry with which fourteenth century knights liked to surround themselves.

The lords and knights of Chaucer's day took their warlike pursuits very seriously, as indeed they had to if they were to win the victories they desired over their French foes. Accordingly, they spent a good deal of time in martial sports in the form of tournaments and jousts. These occasions also provided an excellent opportunity for the untried young warrior to practise his skills before entering a real battlefield. There were elaborate rules governing these events, which by Chaucer's day were staged as much for the entertainment of guests and visitors as for practice. Jousting was a form of combat between two knights each mounted on horseback and armed with shield and lance. Usually, the opposing horsemen galloped toward each other down the lists, or arena, separated by a wooden barrier to stop them colliding head on. As one can imagine, this could be an exceedingly dangerous sport, and

Opposite Caernarvon, another of Edward I's Welsh castles, with part of the old walled city that grew up under its protection

CONWAY CASTLE

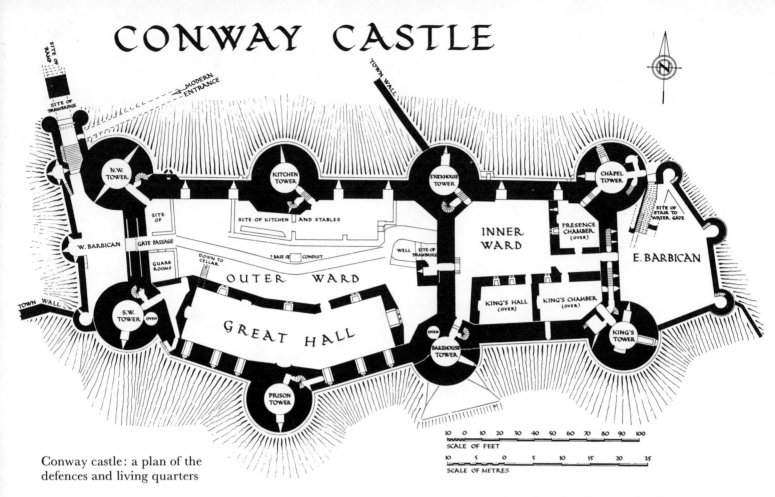

Conway castle: a plan of the defences and living quarters

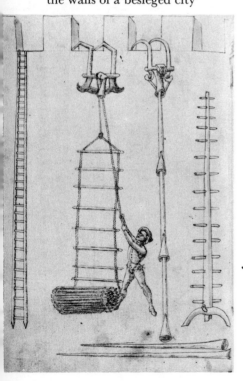

Various devices used to scale the walls of a besieged city

various precautions were taken to avoid undue fatalities. The lists were policed by officials carrying long batons with which to separate the combatants, and the jousts (lances) were usually tipped as an extra protection. Even so, there were many serious casualties. The knights all dressed in their finest armour, their crests and shields emblazoned with their brave coats-of-arms, their helmets splendidly plumed with feathers, and their horses draped in cloths of gold and scarlet and other rich colours. Heralds sounded their trumpets as the charge down the lists commenced.

Another form of combat was the tourney, or *mêlée* in which two opposing bands of knights staged a mock battle, on foot and on horseback. These were, if anything, more dangerous still, and it became necessary to have the knights each swear that he was entering the fray in a friendly spirit, and not in order to settle any private quarrel. Yet many were crushed to death, or trampled and injured by the frightened horses, and in Chaucer's time people still spoke of the time in 1240 when sixty knights were choked and crushed to death at one tournament.

The safest preparation for war, if less exciting, was the *quintain*, which was a movable wooden arm bearing a shield, attached to a post, on which the younger tyros could pour their energies. "Prowess", as Jean Froissart remarked, "is so noble a virtue and of so great a recommendation, that one must never pass over it too briefly, for its is the mother stuff and the light of noble men, and as the log cannot spring to life without fire, so the noble man cannot come to perfect honour, or to the glory of the world without prowess." Some young bloods, no doubt, were fired by dreams of honour or glory; but there must have been as many who were fired by the prospect of rich booty, and the

70

capturing of noble prisoners who could be ransomed for a great fortune. This was the way in which many a young knight established himself.

Many changes were taking place in the dress of knights in Chaucer's lifetime. The old coat of mail, or *hauberk,* no longer gave enough protection, and it was now often reinforced with steel plates worn on the arms, legs and feet. Likewise, steel gauntlets shielded the hands and forearms. Most knights wore a fairly simple conical helmet on their heads, usually without a vizor. But for tournaments and other great occasions it was customary to wear a "tourney" helmet, or *heaume,* which as well as having a vizor often bore a decorative figure perched up on top in the shape of a swan's neck or another animal. The mailcoat, too, was changing. In place of the old type of banded mail – steel rings sewn onto thick linen or velvet – many knights preferred to use chain mail, where the steel rings were interwoven with each other without being sewn onto any lining material. It was lighter, of course, but it was still normally worn over a quilted garment called a *gambeson,* which was padded with wool, and provided extra protection. An interesting description of a knight was given by Chaucer in his *Tale of Sir Topaz:*

Defenders begging for mercy from the victorious attacking army

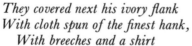

> They covered next his ivory flank
> With cloth spun of the finest hank,
> With breeches and a shirt

Above The attackers and defenders parleying before a beleaguered city

Left Strengthening the walls of a city against attack

A battle between water-borne knights

And over that (in case it fail)
A tunic, then a coat of mail,
    For fear he might be hurt.
And over that contrived to jerk
A hauberk (finest Jewish work
    and strong in every plate)
And over that his coat of arms,
White as a lily flower's charms,
    In which he must debate.

And as to his weapons:

His shield was of a golden red
Emblazoned with a porker's head,
    Carbuncles at the side. . .

Boiled leather on his shins had he,
His sword was sheathed in ivory,
    His helm was copper bright.
His saddle was of narwhal bone,
His bridle shone like precious stone
    Or sun, or moon, at night.

Of cypress was the spear he bore,
Not made for peace but boding war,
    The head was sharply ground. . .

The massive defensive walls of
Harlech castle still stand today

Castles and sieges

Chaucer's England was a land dominated by castles, the greatest of which had been built by King Edward I at the beginning of the century. In the West the great barons and earls whose lands lay on the border with Wales, the "marcher lords" as they were known, held the great castles there to subdue the Welsh, against whom Edward I had fought so bitterly. These included Caernarvon, with its famous walled town that grew up under the shadow of the castle walls; and Beaumaris, which incidentally formed one of the last examples of the old concentric-plan castles, with its inner and outer walls of fortification. London, of course, was dominated by the solidly built Tower of London, erected by William I after his conquest of England in the eleventh century. Many of the great houses in England, too, especially in the more lawless North, were built as semi-fortified residences, designed to withstand a certain amount of attack by siege. Many of them had narrow arrow-shot window slits from which the archers could fire down upon their attackers without exposing themselves to danger, and overlooking a moat which denied access to the house except by a wooden draw-bridge which could be raised in time of attack, and sometimes a heavy iron portcullis lowered behind the gate. Some of the larger fortified houses, like the one built by John of Gaunt, had one or two great stone towers commanding the approaches, on which cannon could be mounted to discourage unwelcome visitors.

One of the finest castles built in the fourteenth century – fewer were being built in Chaucer's day than in earlier generations – was at Bodiam in Sussex, the ruins of which can still be seen today. Licence to build the castle was given by King Edward III to Sir Edward Dalyngrage in 1386, and building commenced soon after. The castle stands four-square, surrounded by a moat filled from a nearby stream. It was entered by a drawbridge, which was lowered from the gate of a stone gatehouse standing flanked by castellated towers on either side. The gateway itself could be closed by stout oak doors. Narrow slits were placed in the towers for the use of the archers, while the defending soldiers at the top of the towers, could pour down boiling liquids onto the heads of the attackers below, using funnels made in the overhanging floors at the top of the towers. Even if the enemy managed to penetrate the moat, drawbridge, and main gate, once inside the courtyard they would still have to face a devastating fire from the defenders still perched on top of their various towers at the corners of the edifice. Inside the castle there were barracks for the garrison, a chapel with a small private room for the priest, and the living quarters for Sir Edward and his household. These consisted of a hall, private chambers, butteries, pantries and the kitchen, and – though one cannot now be certain – a kitchen and dining hall for the soldiers. On the spot where modern tourists now stand taking photographs among the flowers and gardens, one might easily forget that this was once a place where lords and ladies, knights and squires lived and fought, and enjoyed their hunting and falconing beneath the gleaming white walls.

Siege warfare played a prominent part in the fourteenth century campaigns. Although a few primitive cannon were in existence and

Above and below A gold noble issued by Edward III in 1344 to commemorate the victory of the English over the French at Sluys in 1340

If a besieged city was finally taken, the defenders could expect little mercy from the victorious army

The battle between the French and English fleets at Sluys, in 1340, is probably the first of modern naval battles

occasionally used in battle, they had not yet begun to threaten the strength of the medieval castles as one day they would. The methods used in siege warfare differed, in fact, very little from those used by the ancient Romans. A kind of giant catapult known as a *trebuchet* was used to hurl rocks over the parapets of the castle, and tall wooden towers were used by the besiegers to try and scale the walls. At the foot of the walls, miners dug tunnels in an effort to undermine the masonry and bring it crashing down. But the advantage in siege warfare usually lay with the besieged. With plenty of provisions in store, the inmates could fight off the enemy with missiles thrown down from the walls – red-hot iron bars, boiling pitch, quicklime, and heavy pieces of timber, while the archers shot down their arrows or bolts. Mines could sometimes be detected by hanging up large copper basins which were sensitive to the vibrations caused by the tunnellers. Sometimes counter-mines were dug, and if the tunnellers met each other bloody battles were fought in the dark cramped tunnels underground. Sometimes, after a long siege, the successful besiegers would wreak terrible vengeance on those who had held out for so long. The Black Prince, for example, so chivalrous in some respects, carried out a terrible massacre of the occupants – men, women and children – of Limoges Castle after he had finally taken it in 1367, which was in stark contrast to the chivalric ideals to which contemporaries paid so much lip service.

Fighting ships

In an age famous for its knights and its code of chivalry, it is easy to forget that England even then had some naval strength, although it is true that the nation's first full-scale navy was not founded until the reign of Henry VIII (1509–47). The ships of Chaucer's time had not changed much since the previous centuries. The greatest change that had taken place was that the old Viking tradition – and indeed Roman tradition – of long narrow fighting vessels was giving way to a more squat, tub-like warship, the main features of which were the wooden "castles" raised

74

If the English were to fight overseas boats had to transport horses as well as men

up in stem and stern, in which the soldiers awaited their hand-to-hand engagement. The ships had a single mast in the centre of the deck, and a single square sail above which flew the pennant. The men who served in the ships and commanded them were mostly soldiers and knights, who took to the seas as and when necessary. The most decisive campaigns and battles in the Middle Ages took place on the land, not on the sea. The sea was simply a hazard to be negotiated as the soldiers made their way to their landing point, a hazard in which storms and gales and primitive navigation played a greater part than enemy naval presences. It was in tiny ships such as these, no more than a few yards from prow to stern, that the soldiers of Edward III and Richard II crossed the English Channel to fight their campaigns in the Hundred Years' War.

Left Boat-building, an allegorical picture showing Noah constructing the ark

Below During the fourteenth century navigational methods improved, making naval excursions less hazardous

Naval engagements did take place, however, from time to time, as the following account shows, when Edward III encountered a French naval force on his way to the mainland of the Continent. The description is Jean Froissart's. King Edward III "and his army sailed from the Thames, the day before the eve of St. John the Baptist, 1340, and made straight for Sluys. On his way he fell in with the French navy, of which we have been speaking, and though the numbers were four to one against him, resolved to give them battle. The French were equally desirous to engage, and as soon as they were in sight of the English they filled the *Christopher* – the large ship which they had captured but a short time before – with trumpets and other warlike instruments, ordering her to begin the attack. The battle was fierce, murderous and horrible. In the end, the English came off victorious, the *Christopher* was recaptured by them, and all in her taken or killed."

Even in sea-battles the power of the English long-bow (*left*) proved superior to that of the older cross-bow (*right*)

5   *The Black Death*

IN 1348, when Chaucer was probably a boy of eight years old, England suffered the greatest calamity known to her chroniclers for many centuries. This was the Black Death, that great pandemic of bubonic plague prevalent throughout the known world in the fourteenth century, and which in England killed, according to various estimates, between a third and two fifths of the entire population. As we shall see, the Black Death wrought many deep changes in English life, from the style of life on the land, to the subjects taught in the universities. But first we will look at how medieval people sought to protect themselves with their medicine against such horrors.

Medieval medicine

In an age when death was liable to overtake man suddenly, when many sicknesses quickly proved fatal, medieval people turned to God first, and to the physician as a desperate second. If prayer failed, they resorted to the apothecary and physician, and sometimes the surgeon, whose practice of medicine was based upon a peculiar mixture of superstition, astrology, folk remedies, and a bastardization of the medicine practised by the ancient Greeks. A well known character in Chaucer's day was the alchemist, who spent much of his time trying to turn base metals into gold. Chaucer described his stock-in-trade as:

> *Water in rubefaction; bullock's gall,*
> *Arsenic, brimstone, sal ammoniac,*
> *And herbs that I could mention by the sack,*
> *Moonwort, valerian, agrimony and such.*

A doctor prescribed the following remedy for a wound. "Take four pounds of virgin wax, and resolve it in a woman's milk that beareth a knave child." To this should be added "an ounce of mastic and an ounce of frankincense, and let them boil well together till it be well y-mellyd (mixed). . . . Then do it off the fire, and in the doing a down look thou have y-broke half a pound of tormentile well y-powdered all ready, and

Knowledge was so unspecialized in Chaucer's day that one work could include discourses on: theology, canon law, philosophy, medicine and general information. This illustration is from such a work

cast therein, and stir all away without boiling, till it be cold." Next, "Take up that floateth above and smear thine hand with oil or fresh butter, and bear it again to the fire as thou wilt bear wax, till it be well y-mellyd, and do therewith as thou wilt."

In the Middle Ages, death and sickness were often seen as God's punishment for sin, and one should not wonder that many cures involved prayers and incantations, sometimes of a semi-pagan nature. Indeed, the Church found it necessary to forbid the use of such incantations "in the gathering of medicinal herbs, save only with the Creed and the Paternoster in honour of God and our Lord." No doubt this appeal to the Goddess of Nature was one against which the Church would have taken the strongest exception: "Mighty art thou, Queen of the Gods! Thee, O Goddess, I adore in thy Godhead, and on thy name do call. Vouchsafe now to fulfil my prayer, and I will give thee thanks . . . Come to me with thy healing powers!"

In the twelfth century, the doctor had acted as his own chemist and druggist, but by Chaucer's day the apothecary was emerging as a specialist dispenser of drugs and medicines. Scores of shiploads of medical goods were being imported from the great European port of Venice – opium, rhubarb, senna, sugar, camphor, cloves, ginger, pepper, cinnamon, mace and nutmeg. So precious was the cargo, that we read of it being guarded by archers.

Much of medieval medicine was bound up with astrology. Like the physician in *The Canterbury Tales*:

> *No one alive could talk as well as he did*
> *On points of medicine and surgery;*
> *For, being grounded in astronomy*
> *He watched his patient's favourable star*
> *And, by his Natural Magic, knew what are*
> *The lucky hours and planetary degrees*
> *For making charms and magic effigies.*

The physician would consult, too, medieval handbooks on the humours and complexions of the patient, prescribing his remedies accordingly:

> *The cause of every malady you'd got*
> *He knew, and whether dry, cold, moist or hot;*
> *He knew their seat, their humour and condition.*
> *He was a perfect practising physician.*

Often, the doctor worked hand-in-hand with a friendly apothecary, and Chaucer accused them of outright collusion:

> *All his apothecaries in a tribe*
> *Were ready with the drugs he would prescribe,*
> *And each made money from the other's guile;*
> *They had been friendly for a goodish while.*

Many natural substances were thought to work for the good of a patient's health: there was the right substance for the right complaint. As Chaucer archly commented of the physician himself:

> *Gold stimulates the heart, or so we're told.*
> *He therefore had a special love of gold.*

Indeed, the physician's services did not come cheaply,

In blood-red garments, slashed with bluish-grey
And lined with taffeta, he rode his way;
Yet he was rather close as to expenses,
And kept the gold he won in pestilences.

The ordinary medical practitioner of Chaucer's time usually carried with him what can best be described as a "ready reckoner" in which full instructions were given for a patient's treatment, in which among other things diet and surgery were related to astrology. In a tradition which stemmed from ancient classical times, medical science – if one can call it that – was based on the idea that man, like the natural world in which he lived, was composed of the four elements of earth, air, fire and water, and according to the proportions of these various elements in the patient's body his character was sanguine, choleric, phlegmatic or melancholic. In addition, the positions of the planets and "celestial spheres" determined the mysterious fluids which ran through his body, and which in medieval medicine would be treated by blood-letting in various parts of the body. The following is a table from one of the doctor's ready-reckoners, showing how to follow the signs of the zodiac in preparing for surgical treatment:

ARIES Avoid incisions in the head and face, and cut no vein in the head.
TAURUS Avoid incisions in the neck and throat, and cut no vein there.
GEMINI Avoid incisions in the arms or hands and shoulders, and cut no vein.
CANCER Avoid incisions in the breast and sides, lesions in the stomach

Opposite This illustration from a French book on surgery seems to suggest that simple operations on the head were sometimes performed despite the lack of anaesthetic

Dentistry, although of a somewhat
primitive kind, was not unknown.
"Dentists" such as this set up
booths at fairs, extracting teeth
for a small sum

and lungs, and cut no vein that goes to the spleen.

LEO Avoid incisions of the nerves, lesions of the sides and bones, and
do not cut the back either by opening or bleeding.

VIRGO Avoid opening a wound in the belly, and in internal parts.

LIBRA Avoid opening wounds in the umbilicus and parts of the belly
and do not open a vein in the back, or do cupping.

SCORPIO Avoid cutting the testicles, anus, vesica, and do not cut the
vereda in man or woman.

SAGITTARIUS Avoid incisions in the thighs and fingers and do not cut
blemishes or growths.

CAPRICORN Avoid cutting the knees or veins and sinews in these
places.

AQUARIUS Avoid cutting the legs and any place as far as the heels.

PISCES Avoid cutting the feet.

The advantages of blood-letting – "phlebotomy" – were described
by the same writer as follows: it "clears the mind, strengthens the
memory, cleanses the stomach, dries up the brain, warms the marrow,
sharpens the hearing, stops tears, encourages discrimination, develops
the senses, promotes digestion, produces a musical voice, dispels

torpor, drives away anxiety, feeds the blood, rids it of poisonous matter, and brings long life. It eliminates rheumatic ailments, gets rid of pestilent diseases, cures pains, fevers and various sicknesses, and makes the urine clean and clear." And just in case this torrent of blood-letting failed to have the promised result, "put hot leaves of *hyosciamus* moistened with oil near or over the affected place." It is extraordinary to think that the practice of blood-letting, and the use of leeches – fished out of rivers and streams – persisted right up to the twentieth century. In the mid-fourteenth century, England was ill-prepared for the calamity which was soon to overtake her.

The Scourge from the East

The Black Death came like a scourge from the East, which in Chaucer's day was also the source of spices, silks and many other worldly pleasures. Few Englishmen ever saw the East for themselves, and consequently most of the descriptions we have of the origin of the plague in those parts are vividly embroidered by the writers' imagination. For example, one Flemish priest who had received a letter from a friend at the papal court in Rome spoke of "horrors and unheard of tempests" which had overtaken India. "On the first day," he said, "there was a rain of frogs, serpents, lizards, scorpions, and many venomous beasts of that sort. On the second, thunder was heard, and lightning and sheets of fire fell upon the earth, mingled with hail stones of marvellous size, which slew almost all, from the greatest even to the least. On the third day there fell fire from heaven and stinking smoke, which slew all that were left of men and beasts, and burned up all the cities and towns in those parts." The priest added that the infection was rapidly spread by the wind. "By these tempests the whole province was infected, and it is conjectured that, through the foul blast of wind that came from the South, the whole seashore and surrounding lands were infected, and are waxing more and more poisonous from day to day."

The feeling that the plague was God's punishment for the way in which society had fallen into evil paths – the priests lax, the merchants usurious – is perhaps reflected in the belief that it seemed to originate from the heavens. For apart from the "rain of frogs, serpents, lizards" spoken of by the Flemish priest, there was also "a vast rain of fire" said to have fallen between Cathay and Persia, "falling in flakes like snow, and burning up mountains and plains and other lands, with men and women. And then arose vast masses of smoke, and whosoever beheld this died within the space of half a day, and likewise any man or woman who looked upon those who had seen this."

In 1346 and 1347 many rumours of this kind were circulating yet no one really knew where or how the plague had begun. According to the contemporary chronicler, Knighton, it broke out first in India, "and spread thence in Tharsis, thence to the Saracens, and at last to the Christians and Jews." He added, "In the space of a single year, namely from Easter to Easter, as it was rumoured at the court of Rome, eight thousand legions of men perished in those distant regions, besides Christians."

No doubt the plague spread northward and westward into Europe – not by the great winds of which chroniclers spoke – but by the trade routes, especially those by which merchants brought their Eastern spices and silks in their galleys from ports in the Crimea to the Mediterranean – Genoa, Messina, and of course Venice. For the "Black Death", as the pestilence soon became known, was in fact bubonic plague, a disease whose carriers were the fleas of rats, hundreds and thousands of which scurried about in the gloomy holds of the merchant ships and in the sewers and garbage-filled streets of the towns and cities of the fourteenth century. We can be almost sure of this from the tell-tale mark of the *bubo*, an inflammation of the lymphatic glands which manifested itself in the groin or armpit of the victim.

A great byproduct of the Black Death was Boccaccio's famous collection of stories, the *Decameron*, which were supposed to have been told to one another by a group of Florentine ladies and gentlemen to pass the time while seeking refuge from the plague in a villa outside Florence. In this book, Boccaccio referred to the "emergence of certain tumours in the groin or the armpits, some of which grew as large as a common apple, others as an egg, some more, some less, which the common folk called *gavocciolo*. From the two said parts of the body this deadly *gavocciolo* soon began to propagate, and spread itself in all directions indifferently [indiscriminately] after which the form of malady began to change, black spots or livid making their appearance in many cases on the arm or thigh or elsewhere, now few and large, now minute and numerous."

Some writers noted a more virulent form of the plague – pneumonic plague – in which the sufferer also contracted pneumonia, mainly in the months between late winter and early spring. As a contemporary noted, it involved "continuous fever, but with apostumes and carbuncles on the external parts, principally on the armpits and groin. From this one died in five days." He added, "Men suffer in their lungs and breathing and whoever have these corrupted, or even slightly attacked, cannot by any means escape nor live beyond two days."

The Italian author of the *Decameron*, who witnessed the plague himself, wrote that its virulence was the greater because "intercourse was apt to convey it from the sick to the whole, just as fire devours things dry or greasy when they are brought close to it." Indeed, "The evil went further, for not merely by speech or association with the sick was the malady communicated to the healthy with consequent peril of common death; but any that touched the clothes of the sick, or aught else that had been touched or used by them, seemed thereby to contract the disease." Neither prayer nor penance was any use in stemming the fearful and inevitable advance of the shadow of death. "Some were tormented with abscesses in various parts of their body, and from these many, by means of lancing, or with long suffering, recovered. Others had small black pustules scattered over the whole surface of their body, from which very few, nay, scarcely a single person, returned to life and health."

According to Robert of Avesbury, the Black Death first reached the coast of England in August, 1348. "It began in England in the neigh-

The doctor of physic was another of Chaucer's pilgrims, but, as his science was "grounded in astronomy", he was probably not much help to his patients

bourhood of Dorchester, about the Feast of St. Peter ad Vinculas . . . immediately spreading rapidly from place to place . . . Many persons who were healthy in the early morning, before midday were snatched from human affairs. It permitted none whom it marked down to live more than three or four days, without choice of persons, save only in the case of a few rich people. On the same day of their death, the bodies of twenty, forty, sixty and many times more persons were delivered to the Church's burial in the same pit."

The Chronicle of the Greyfriars at Lynn, in East Anglia, put the start of the plague a little earlier, in June. It spoke of two ships, one of which was from Bristol, which anchored in the port of Melcombe in Dorset. "One of the sailors had brought with him from Gascony the seeds of the terrible pestilence and, through him, the men of that town of Melcombe were the first in England to be infected." It is possible that

In matutino interficiebam omn[e]
peccatores terre : ut disperderem de

One medieval artist's view of the plague

the ship in question had come from the Channel Islands. King Edward III had already written to the Governor of Jersey on the subject of the pestilence, which was already raging there, because of this, and the high mortality among the fishing folk of the island, "our rent for the fishing which has yearly been paid us cannot now be obtained without the impoverishing and excessive oppression of those fishermen still left." This was a pattern which soon was to be repeated a thousand-fold within England itself, bringing in its wake a range of acute economic problems.

The major ports of Southampton and Bristol soon fell victim to the plague. Knighton wrote that "there perished almost the whole strength of the town, as it were surprised by sudden death." Once infected, few lived more than two or three days in their beds, sick and hopeless, with nothing that the local physicians could do with all their star-gazing, herbal remedies, bleeding and prayers. "Then this cruel death spread on all sides, following the course of the sun."

Rapidly, the plague spread up from the south coast, claiming most of the residents of the sea ports in Dorset and the region thereabouts. Local people began to take drastic precautions, putting their towns into a virtual state of self-imposed siege. As one Geoffrey le Baker recalled, the plague "raged so violently throughout Devon and Somerset as far as Bristol that the people of Gloucester would not let those of Bristol come into their parts, for they all thought that the breath of persons who lived among those who were thus dying was infected." But it was no use; there was no holding the deadly infection: "At length it invaded Gloucester, London and at last the whole of England, with such violence that scarcely one person in ten of either sex survived." Geoffrey le

Baker exaggerated wildly, but it was nevertheless true that at least a third of the population perished; more in some localities – no doubt those which like Oxford lay at the centre of communications by road – and a lesser proportion in more isolated areas.

We have many accounts of the progress of the pestilence from the records of the dioceses. The Church was a great employer of men, not only as priests and clerks, but as a great landlord, with hundreds of manors all over the country; and it derived its income from rents, tithes and produce all of which were directly dependent upon the presence of men to do the work. In January the following year, 1349, the Bishop of Bath and Wells, Ralph of Shrewsbury, sent a letter to all the priests in his diocese, which vividly shows the damage that was being done to the fabric of life:

"The contagious pestilence of the present day, which is spreading far and wide, has left many parish churches and other livings in our diocese without parson or priest to care for their parishioners. Since no priests can be found who are willing . . . to take on the pastoral care of these aforesaid places, nor to visit the sick and administer to them the Sacraments of the Church (perhaps for fear of infection and contagion), we understand that many people are dying without the Sacrament of Penance. These people have no idea what resources are open to them in such a case of need and believe that, whatever the straits they may be in, no confession of their sins is useful or meritorious unless it is made to a duly ordained priest."

The Bishop stressed that, in view of the enormous mortality, the priests must act quickly and effectively to provide for the salvation of the souls of those who had wandered into the paths of error. He therefore strictly commanded "the rectors, vicars and parish priests in all your churches, and you, the deans elsewhere in your deaneries where the comfort of a priest is denied the people, that . . . you should at once publicly command and persuade all men . . . that, if they are on the point of death and cannot secure the services of a priest, then they should make confession to each other . . . whether to a layman or, if no man is present, then even to a woman."

These were desperate measures to be taken by a Church normally so jealous of guarding the privileges of its clergy. The Bishop added that he realized that many folk might fear that their confessions, made to laymen, would be broadcast for malicious reasons. He therefore urged his priests "in the bowels of Jesus Christ" to make it quite clear that all who "might hear confessions in this way, that they are bound by the laws of the Church to conceal and keep secret such confessions, and that they are prohibited by sacred canonical decrees from betraying such confessions by word, sign, or any other means, except at the wish of those who have made such confession. If they break this law then they should know that they commit a most grievous sin and, in so doing, incur the wrath of Almighty God and of the whole Church."

The shortage of priests posed a problem in other respects, too. Bishop Ralph found it necessary even to relax the rules concerning the administration of the Sacraments. For example, when no priest was available, he authorized the Eucharist to be administered by a deacon.

And even more desperate, "if there is no priest to administer the Sacrament of extreme Unction, then, as in other matters, faith must suffice."

So many people had died by mid-1349 that burials began to present a problem, for the large mass graves that had become necessary were clearly a hazard to the health of the rest of the community. The Bishop of Worcester decided to ban any further burials in his Cathedral churchyard, and opened a new one in the city of Worcester. He noted mournfully that "the burials have in these days, to our sorrow, increased," and that he wished to provide the best remedy against "the corruption of the bodies."

The plague in London

It was not long before the plague reached the capital. A meeting of Parliament was delayed, in order to reduce the risk of infection, and many people fled to the countryside, hoping in the fresh air and isolation to remove themselves from the shadow of death. Often they received a hostile reception, like the people who had fled from Bristol hoping to find sanctuary in nearby Gloucester. From time to time, the government had tried to clean up London. It is true that Chaucer's contemporaries knew little of the dangers of poor hygiene, and certainly did little about it; but pollution was certainly a subject in the mind of the government even at this early date, and with good reason. The sewers, such as there were, were open ditches which stank to heaven; virtually no houses had any kind of plumbing (which was considered the ultimate refinement of wealth), and garbage was tossed indiscriminately out into the street where it ran down a central gutter.

In 1309 Edward II had sought to do something about the problem of filth: "Seeing that the people in the town do cause the ordure that has been collected in their houses, to be carried and placed in the streets, and in the lanes of the City, whereas they ought to have it carried to the Thames, or elsewhere out of the town; and that thereby the streets and lanes are more encumbered than they used to be, we do forbid, on the King's behalf, that from henceforth any person shall have the ordure that has been collected in his house, carried into the King's highways; but let them cause the same to be carried to the Thames, or elsewhere out of the City, whither it used to be carried." Anyone who defied the regulation was to be *amerced* (fined) forty pence for the first offence, and half a mark (sixteen shillings and eightpence) for each subsequent offence.

According to Robert of Avesbury, the Black Death raged on London for almost a year, from the autumn of 1348 until the summer of the next year. "Reaching London about the Feast of All Saints, it slew many persons daily. . . . In a newly made cemetery in Smithfield the bodies of more than two hundred persons, besides those that were buried in other cemeteries of the same city, were buried every day." Smithfield in Chaucer's day was an open space just outside the city, which was brought into use for these mass burials.

The pestilence was no respecter of persons. Many contemporaries

commented on its "injustice", for it "seized especially the young and strong, commonly sparing the elderly and feeble. Scarcely any one ventured to touch the sick, and healthy persons shunned the once, and still, precious possessions of the dead as infectious. People perfectly well on one day were found dead on the next."

The Black Death took a particularly high toll in London, as one might expect, with its dense overcrowding, and its poor sanitation, and its identity as a centre of communications by road and by sea. Probably 30,000 Londoners perished out of a total population of 70,000. Surely this was God's punishment for the sins of the community. For London was seen by many as the embodiment of evil – its dedication to the pursuit of wealth, its defiance of the sumptuary laws which demanded that men should not dress above their station.

A deep feeling of remorse overtook the capital, like the rest of the country. Knighton recalled that about the time of Michaelmas in 1349, more than a hundred men, mostly from the Low Countries, came to London "And twice a day, sometimes in the Church of St. Paul, sometimes in other places of the City, in sight of all the people, covered with a linen cloth from the thighs to the heels, the rest of the body being bare, and each wearing a cap marked before and behind with a red cross, and holding a scourge with three thongs having each a knot through which sharp points were fixed, went barefoot in procession one after another, scourging their bare and bleeding bodies.

"Four of them would sing in their own tongue, all the others making response, in the manner of litanies sung by Christians. Three times in their procession all together would fling themselves upon the ground, their hands outspread in the form of a cross, continually singing. And beginning with the last, one after another, as they lay, each in turn struck the man before him once with his flail; and so from one to another, each performed the same rite to the last. Then each resumed his usual garments, and still wearing their caps and holding their flails, they returned to their lodging. And it was said that they performed the same penance every evening."

The Archbishop of York, William de la Zouche, issued a stern call to repentance before it was too late. "In so far as the life of men upon earth is warfare," he proclaimed, "it is no wonder that those who battle amidst the wickedness of the world are sometimes disturbed by uncertain events" – an understatement, perhaps, of the Black Death. He added, "For Almighty God sometimes allows those whom he loves to be chastened so that their strength can be made complete by the outpouring of spiritual grace in their time of infirmity." Everybody knew, he said, of the pestilence that was endangering England's very life. "This, surely, must be caused by the sins of men who, made complacent by their prosperity, forget the bounty of the most high Giver."

At last the plague abated, almost as suddenly as it had come. To Chaucer's contemporaries it must have seemed that no further damage could possibly be done, short of the world coming to an end. All over England churches lay empty of priests and congregations; the churchyards were overflowing with graves; and in the countryside the fields lay empty and neglected, the harvests rotting, farm implements rusting, and the forest and waste beginning to reclaim the edges of the cultivated land. If the Black Death was seen by many Englishmen of the time as God's chastisement of sinners, designed to bring them back from their paths of error, they were soon to be disillusioned even more. For the Black Death had accelerated deep social changes the seeds of which had already been sown in rural England, and which were in many respects to bring to an end the ancient servile basis of rural life. Medieval feudalism as it had existed for many centuries before was to prove one of the greatest casualties of the pestilence.

6   *After the Pestilence*

LARGE PARTS of the countryside were virtually depopulated where the pestilence had taken its greatest toll. Villages and hamlets lay still and empty in the shadow of death. Gentlefolk could not find servants for their households, and sheep and cattle strayed without herdsmen to tend them, and "all things were left with none to care for them." The Black Death had wrought untold destruction on every form of human life and institution. William Dene, a monk of Rochester, described how the plague had decimated his bishop's household. He "lost four priests, five esquires, ten attendants, seven young clerics and six pages so that nobody was left to serve him in any capacity." At Malling, the bishop had consecrated two new abbesses, but both had died almost at once, leaving only four nuns and four novices. William Dene added, "To our great grief the plague carried off so vast a multitude of the people of both sexes that nobody could be found who would bear the corpses to the grave." Men and women, he noted, carried their own dead children to the mass graves and flung them down. "From these pits such an appalling stench was given off that scarcely anyone dared even to walk beside the cemeteries."

And on the land farming was, for the time being at least, ruined. "All the labourers, skilled or unskilled, were so carried away by the spirit of revolt that neither King, nor law, nor justice, could restrain them." The Black Death spelled a bad time for landlords. With the great mortality, there were no longer enough villeins and tenants to farm the fields. Bishop Haymo of Rochester, for example, survived the Black Death, but in all his manors the buildings began to fall into decay, and there were hardly any manors which returned as much as £100 in rents as once they had. In the monastery at Rochester itself, supplies ran short, and the monks had great difficulty in getting enough to eat. Indeed, they had either to grind their own bread or go without. But a contemporary noted sourly, "The prior, however, ate everything of the best."

In 1352, the patrons of two local churches at Great Colington and Little Colington made a petition to the Bishop of Hereford to unite the

two livings, since "the sore calamity of pestilence ... has so reduced the number of the people of the said churches, and [there] still exists such a paucity of labourers and other inhabitants, such manifest sterility of the lands, and such notorious poverty in the said parishes, that the parishioners and receipts of both churches scarcely suffice to support one priest."

Knighton wrote, too, of the great murrain (epidemic) of sheep everywhere in the kingdom; in one place alone 5,000 sheep died in a single pasture. The corpses lay rotting, so that neither bird nor beast would go near them. Also, "There was great cheapness of all things, owing to the general fear of death, since very few people took any account of riches or poverty of any kind." No doubt some with a more extreme view of God's vengeance would have applauded this. But a horse that was once worth forty shillings would now only fetch six or seven, a fat ox four shillings, a cow twelve pence, a heifer sixpence, a fat wether fourpence, a sheep threepence, a lamb twopence, a large pig fivepence. And a stone (14 pounds) of wool was now only worth nine-pence.

In the autumn following the Black Death, even the payment of higher wages did not attract enough men to come and reap the harvest. "A reaper was not to be had for less than eight pence, with his food," nor "a mower for less than ten pence, with his food." Knighton sorrowed that "many crops rotted in the fields for want of men to gather them," and that unlike the famine conditions sometimes known in earlier times, "there was so great an abundance of all kinds of corn that they were scarcely regarded."

The great men of the land and other lords who had tenants remitted

Birds were a perpetual nuisance stealing grain from the fields. Slings and stones was one way of getting rid of them

the payment of their rents, lest the tenants should go away – "some half their rents, some more, some less, some for one, two or three years according as they could come to an agreement." Never before in the history of the English countryside had the enterprising tenant farmer and villein – those that survived, at least – had such an excellent opportunity to strengthen their social position. Knighton added that the same process took place with the lowlier farm workers, those who paid their rents in labour. The landlords "were obliged to relieve and remit these services, either excusing them entirely, or taking them on easier terms, in the form of a small rent, lest their houses should be irreparably ruined and the land should remain uncultivated. And all sorts of food became excessively dear." In these greatly changed circumstances, the landlords had to improve in a way they had never been forced to before. The Prior of Durham, for example, in 1366 had to agree a lower rent for his tenants until he could find a tenant prepared to pay more. "One messuage and three oxgangs of land, which had been Nicholas Ben's, are signed to William Smyth, John of Heswell and Robert Dines, to have and to hold until another tenant who shall be willing to take the land and pay the old rent, *viz.* forty shillings per annum. . . . And be it known that they shall pay, for the first three years, by his grace, thirty shillings per annum."

In Chaucer's time, many villeins had already been commuting their services to their landlords for money payments, and slowly changing their status from peasants to rent-payers. The advantages to the villein were that he need not bother to help the lord for example at harvest time, when he had harvest of his own to take in. The advantage to the lord was that he could use the money to hire labourers who would work directly for him, and from whom he could extract more effort without the distractions of the labourers having land of their own to work. After the Black Death, wage levels began to rise at a tremendous rate, sometimes doubling and even trebling. The Statute of Labourers which the government enacted three years later was a desperate attempt to limit wage levels to the pre-1348 levels, but it had little or no effect. In the new climate, the villeins pressed harder than ever to have their labour services commuted for cash. Beleaguered by mounting household expenses, the landlords were often only too eager to accept in order to raise funds to hire labourers to stave off bankruptcy. By the time of Chaucer's death in 1400, the old-fashioned villeinage with its labour services and remittance of goods in kind was rapidly disappearing, and the place of the old villein class being taken by the rent-paying copyholder and wage-earning labourer. Also, many lords now found it impossible to farm so much demesne lands – which once had accounted for as much as a third of their property – since the cost of labour was too high. Instead, they preferred to let off part of this land to the local tenants on a simple rental basis. As John Burnett has written in his *History of the Cost of Living*, "The Black Death had brought the cost of living for the first time into the forefront of public consideration and concern."

After the Black Death, the poorest class in the country were the wage-earners, the tenant farmer, as we have seen, had the chance of building up his land-holding, and at least the villein who had commuted his labour services for rent was able to live off his own produce. The wage-earner, on the other hand, often had to plough the land without any payment of corn in kind, and his cash payment, measured in a few pence for each day he worked, was quickly eaten away by the inflation that dominated the English economy after the pestilence. Even this pittance

Villeins cutting hay for their lord

England was thickly wooded in Chaucer's time and timber provided fuel, building materials, furniture and many domestic and farm implements

was not a secure livelihood, for the landlord who employed him could dismiss him as quickly as he had hired him. There must have been many thousands of people in England in the later fourteenth century whose plight was similar to that of the "poor plowman" described by William Langland:

> *And as I went by the way, weeping for sorrow,*
> *I saw a poor man by me on the plough hanging.*
> *His coat was of a clout that cary (coarse cloth) was called;*
> *His hood was full of holes, and his hair cut,*
> *With his nobby shoes patched full thick,*
> *His tongue peeped out as he the earth trod,*
> *His hosen overhung his gaiter on every side*
> *All beslobbered in mire as he the plough followed.*
> *Two mittens so scanty made all of patches,*

Right Two of Edward III's gold coins: (*left*) the florin issued in 1344, and (*right*) a noble of 1360–69

Opposite Illuminated manuscript page, showing villeins cutting fire-wood, their main winter task

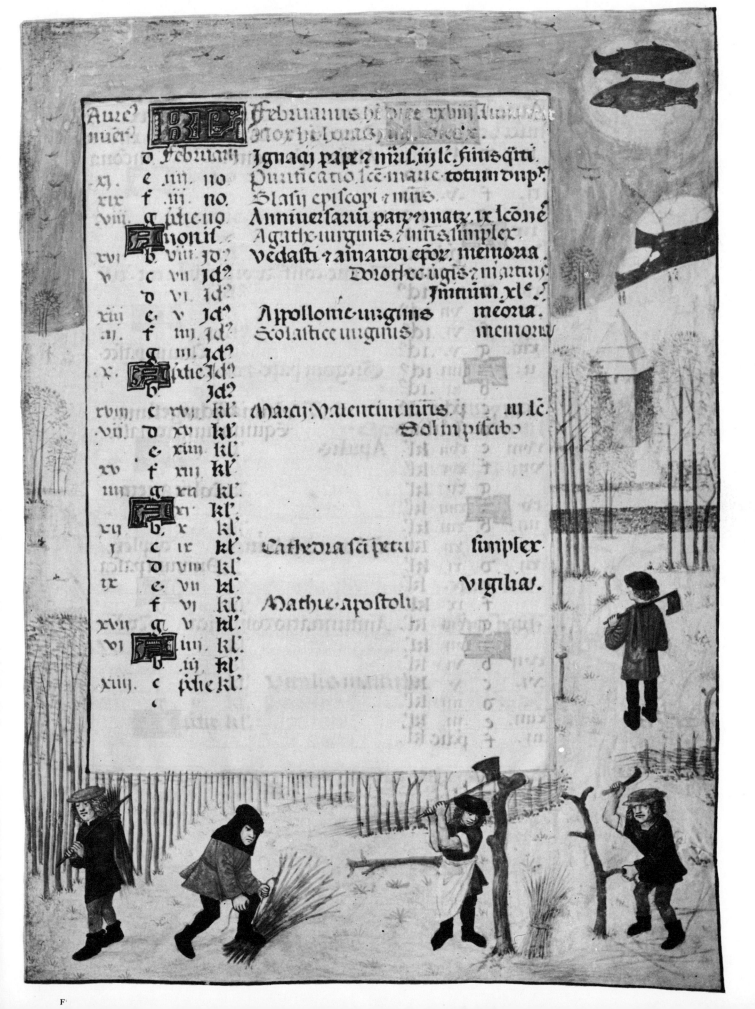

The fingers were worn and full of mud hung.
This fellow wandered in the muck almost to the ankle,
Four heifers before him that weak had become;
You could count all their ribs, so wretched they were;
His wife walked by him with a long goad,
In a coat cut short, cut full high,
Wrapped in a winnowing sheet to cover her from the weather,
Barefoot on the bare ice that the blood followed,
And at the field end lay a little bowl
And on it lay a little child wrapped in rags
And two of two years old on another side
And all they sang a song that was sad to hear
They all cried a cry, a note full of care.
The poor man sighed sore and said, "Children be still."

Although there was no personal income tax or estate duty in the Middle Ages, taxation was a common – and extremely unpopular – feature of life for all classes. Whenever a tenant inherited an estate, however small, he had to pay a fine or relief to his lord, depending on the value of the estate. This applied all the way down the social scale from the greatest lords paying money to the king, to the humblest villein paying a fine on inheriting a cow. There were other taxes, too. Many lords charged high sums of money for manumission, the act by which a villein was made a free man. Many towns were collectively taxed each year with a "farm rent" which guaranteed that its civic liberties would be continued under its charter. The king raised money by his "tenths" and "fifteenths" which each householder in the counties and boroughs had to pay on their estates. But the most unpopular tax of all was the occasional poll tax. That of 1380 levied one shilling on "every person in the kingdom, male or female, of an age of fifteen, of what rank or condition soever, except beggars." For the rich it was an irritant; for the poor a heavy burden. It was paid "with great grudging and many a bitter curse" and did much to ignite the Peasants' Revolt of the following year.

The rich were expected to show charity to the poor for whom they were responsible, especially after the Black Death. Many noblemen provided a daily distribution of food and money to the poor at their gate, usually a few pence each day. John of Gaunt was especially generous: apart from such distributions, in 1372 he sent the poor lazars of Leicester three cartloads of wood for winter fuel, and a tun of Gascony wine for the prisoners in Newgate Gaol. Such charity could provide

Although the medieval kings of England were titular heads of state, the power of the individual monarch depended very largely on his own strength of character. Richard II, seen here receiving a gift from a subject, lost his throne and crown because he was not sufficiently strong

valuable windfalls for the poor, but in general it was of a capricious character.

Government economic policy, so far as it existed in the Middle Ages, was largely determined by feelings of fairness and natural justice rather than pure economic considerations, of which it was generally ignorant. As a modern historian has written, "A code of mercantile ethics, based ultimately on the precepts of the Church, decreed that craftsmen should make their goods honestly and well, that sellers should give good weight and be satisfied with reasonable profits." Many aspects of the medieval economy were subject to regulations. Nationally, there were the Assizes of Bread, Ale and Cloth which sought to control the price and quality of these staple items; and locally there were many similar attempts at control, where the leading merchants and burgesses were able, often effectively, to maintain high standards in the trades and crafts. These policies came to seem all the more important in the inflation which overtook the country after the Black Death.

Law and order

An immediate, and perhaps inevitable result of the Black Death, was a rapid deterioration of law and order, a process which was to culminate in 1381 in that great popular uprising known as the Peasants' Revolt. Contemporary court records and other sources are full of instances of crimes specifically linked with the social disorder brought in the wake of the plague.

Among the clergy, as among the laity, William of Dene found a decline in moral standards. People were "ever more depraved, more prone to every vice and more inclined than before to evil and wickedness." And priests began to take themselves off to where they could get richer stipends than in their own benefices – exploiting the demand for clergy following the mortality. "Day by day the dangers to soul both in clergy and people multiplied." The Church, as we have seen, found itself facing an acute shortage of priests. Knighton noted "everywhere so great a scarcity of priests that many churches were left destitute, without divine service, masses, matins, vespers or sacraments." He remarked that now a chaplain was hardly to be had for less than £10 a year, or priests for £20, double what they might have accepted before. Soon, "vast numbers of men whose wives had died in the pestilence flocked to take orders, many of whom were illiterate, and as it were mere laymen, save so far as they could read a little, although without understanding." What hope was there for maintaining Christian standards of morality in medieval England if the Church itself was unable to maintain a good example? As we read in *Piers Plowman*:

> *Parsons and parish priests complained them to the bishop*
> *That their parishes were poor since the pestilence-time,*
> *To have a licence and a leave at London for to dwell,*
> *And singen there for simony: for silver is sweet.*

Education and language

The Black Death brought changes, too, in English education. Thousands of the clergy, who had formerly acted as teachers and tutors, had perished. One of the most significant changes for the future was the decline of the teaching of Latin, and the more common use of English in place of Norman-French. A contemporary, John Trevisa, attributed much of the change to the work of John Cornwall, a grammar school master, "so that now in the year of our Lord 1385 . . . in all the grammar schools of England children leave French and construe and learn in English." It was in this climate of change that Geoffrey Chaucer composed the *Canterbury Tales*, which can claim to be the first major work in the English language, and the foundation of modern English literature. Trevisa remarked that the young scholars now had "an advantage on one side, and a disadvantage on the other. The advantage is that they learn their grammar in less time than children once did. The disadvantage is that now children of grammar schools no more understand French than their left heel, and that is harmful for them if they should cross the sea and work in strange lands." He added that gentlemen who were fathers now had their work cut out to teach their children the gentle tongue of French themselves, at home. The official seal on this change of tongue was set by an Act of Parliament of 1362 which ordained that in future all legal business was to be pleaded and transacted in English instead of French as before. A further gain to education was that many new colleges and schools were founded to train new scholars to replace those who had died. Simon Islip, Archbishop of Canterbury, founded Canterbury College at Oxford, explaining that it was because "those who are truly learned and accomplished in every kind of learning have largely been exterminated in the epidemics."

Three villeins at work weeding a field, with forked sticks and hoes,
while a woman carries away a bundle of grain she has gleaned

Villeins pruning fruit trees with a special pruning tool like a small
sickle

7 Towards Revolt

THE JUDICIAL SYSTEM of Chaucer's England had as its apex the King, the Privy Council and Parliament. Below them there functioned three courts. These were the Court of Common Pleas, which heard disputes between one subject and another, and which corrected errors in the lower courts. The second was the King's Bench Court, which looked into cases which were of special interest to the King. The third was the Court of Exchequer, which dealt with a range of matters that would today come under the heading of local government, for example the local raising of revenues for the crown, with all the disputes which this entailed. In an age of general lawlessness, which periodically erupted into riots and even rebellion, the first task of any King was to maintain the peace, and for this much depended on whether the monarch had a strong or a weak character. The local instruments of the three central courts were the judges who travelled around the counties of England on assize.

The justices of the peace, so familiar in local justice in Britain today, had their origins in the years shortly before Chaucer's birth. It had been the practice of the crown from time to time to appoint special commissioners to deal with specific problems of government in local areas. An Act of 1327 had given statutory backing to the "keepers of the peace" who had often been commissioned in this way before. These "keepers" were generally members of the local gentry and squirearchy, who as landholders and employers in the villages and hamlets were naturally looked to by the government in the job of arresting suspects, and inquiring into felonies and trespasses. But there their job ended. They were only empowered to investigate complaints; they could not issue judgements. In any case, the support of the sheriff, or shire-reeve, was not always forthcoming to help officials whose status was far from clear.

When Chaucer was a boy there was a considerable debate taking place about the best method of law enforcement. Sir Geoffrey Scrope, then Chief Justice of the King's Bench, wanted to see a team of specially-commissioned royal justices who would have power to travel about the

After the harvest, grain had to be threshed to separate the ears from the straw. Two villeins use wooden flails to do this, while another winnows the grain to get rid of the chaff

Most villages had their own little prison into which miscreants could be put. Petty offences were punished with a time in the stocks, where everyone could see and jeer the wrongdoer

country and try every kind of offence. Scrope felt that their efforts would produce a substantial revenue in fines for the royal exchequer, which at that time was in dire need of funds. The House of Commons, on the other hand, representing the interests of the gentry of the countryside and the burgesses of the towns, wanted to see more power given to their own class. In 1361, twenty years before the Black Death, the problem was more or less resolved, with the old-style "keepers of the peace" being transformed into "justices of the peace," their powers extended from merely inquiring into offences to actually dealing with them as magistrates. In the face of periodical pressure from the Commons, the central government gradually extended the power of the new justices even further afield, into economic and administrative matters, although from time to time it still reverted to the use of special commissioners in time of social unrest, for example in the six or seven years following the Peasants' Revolt of 1381. To many contemporaries, it merely seemed that one more official had been added to the already complicated mosaic of local life.

Each local bench of justices contained a few lay magnates, but in the main they were composed of country gentry with a few lawyers. It was natural that the gentry, represented in the Commons, should wish to provide the justices from their own class, and in Chaucer's lifetime they put some pressure to have the selections made by Parliament. But by the end of the fourteenth century it was generally the practice that the justices should be appointed by the central government, although influence in the shires naturally had an effect.

The number of justices at work in Chaucer's day was small. In 1338 Somerset had only four, and in 1362 Staffordshire and Suffolk three.

A source of grievance to many villeins was the fact that they had to use the lord's mill to grind their corn, and pay for doing so

The man of law, who travelled round his district from assize to assize bringing the rule of the country's law into the lives of the ordinary people

But an Act of 1388 raised the minimum to six justices per county, and two years later this was raised again to eight. The first time we hear of a clerk to the justices is in 1380, when the justices were instructed to swear their oath of service to their clerk "to conceal the counsel of the King, and to perform his duties loyally." The justices were paid four shillings a day while they were at Quarter Sessions, and their clerks two shillings a day. Peers who were justices received no pay, nor was there any other pay for the many other administrative duties the justices had.

These Quarter Sessions took place four times a year, as their name suggests, and formed a landmark in the local calendar. With the justices, clerks, prisoners, juries, friends and relations the average Quarter Sessions probably involved a hundred people, and to accommodate this large number the sessions were often held in a castle in the shire, for example at York, Canterbury, Winchester and Worcester. Elsewhere the Sessions were held in a large inn. The Sessions provided a useful opportunity, in this age of poor communications, for the government to have the latest statutes read out to the assembled throng, before there followed the reading of the charges to the jurors. Generally speaking, the Sessions were conducted with decorum, and all legal formalities were observed – the swearing of the juries, the reading of the indictments, the hearing of the evidence, the bringing in of the verdict, and the passing of the sentence. Parliament made a vigorous protest about the events at one Quarter Sessions in Warwickshire, where the Duke of Clarence who was sitting on the Bench managed to have one poor unfortunate woman tried, convicted and hanged all on the same day.

The most common theme running through the records of the Quarter Sessions meticulously compiled by the clerks in Chaucer's day was violence; and it was a violence that pervaded almost every aspect of life. Quite apart from the routine brawling, drunkenness and assault cases, there were cases of violence involving knights and monks, often in churches during services, which give the lie to the picture of gentility so often made by contemporary writers like Jean Froissart. After all, crime prevention was virtually nil, and no doubt many people in all stations of society from the poorest villein to the greatest nobleman were accustomed to getting their way by force and cunning. Perhaps these were the disreputable folk depicted by a contemporary as gamesters, frequenters of taverns, and "sleepers by day and watchers by night who eat well and drink well, yet have nothing." Among the offences chronicled in the records were arson, rape, robbery, house-breaking, cutting down a hanged woman before she was dead, diverting a watercourse, killing a dog, stealing a corpse from a church, stockpiling corn for profit, brewers and other tradesmen using illicit measures and weights, poaching, and workmen breaking their contracts of employment.

Peasant discontent

The French chronicler Jean Froissart wrote, "It is the custom in England, as in other countries, for the nobility to have great power over the common people, who are their serfs. This means that they are bound by law and custom to plough the fields of their masters, harvest the corn,

The growing discontent of the poor during the fourteenth century is shown in this view of "the courtiers amassing riches at the expense of the poor"

gather it into barns, and thresh and winnow the grain. They must also mow and carry home the hay, cut and collect wood, and perform all manner of tasks of this kind. The peasants have to perform these duties by law."

But the Black Death had thrown an increasing strain on the old ways of doing things. So many peasants and tenants had died that landlords found extreme difficulty either in getting labourers to work in their fields, or in finding tenants to take them off their hands. Landowners protested violently at those peasants and villeins who sought to exploit the situation after the Black Death. One of them was John Gower, who had been a prosperous small landowner before. "Three things," he complained, "all of the same sort, are merciless when they get the upper hand – a water flood, a wasting fire, and the common multitude of small folk." None of them, he wrote, would be checked by reason or discipline. "Ha! Age of Ours! Whither turnest thou, for the poor and small folk, who should cleave to their labour, demand to be better fed than their masters!" And contrary to social custom of the time, "they bedeck them-

The Black Death drastically reduced the number of villeins available to work the land

selves in fine colours and fine attire, whereas were it not for their pride and privy conspiracies, they would be clad in sackcloth as of old.''

Gower condemned them for seeking extortionate wages, complaining that the shepherd and cowherd now demanded more than the head bailiff. These peasants, he added, never tasted wheat bread in the old days. They made their bread either of corn or beans, and drank water from the spring. "Then was the world of such folk well ordered in its estate." To Gower, the peasants worked little, dressed and fed themselves like their masters, while the latter seemed to be sunk in lethargy. "Thus they suffer this nettle, that is so violent in itself, to grow." He added, prophetically, that whoever surveyed the land might well fear that "this impatient nettle will suddenly sting us before men do justice upon it."

A royal ordinance of 1349 tried to fix wages at the 1346 level. Edward III remarked that lately a great part of the people, especially servants, had died during the pestilence, and that some, seeing the pressing needs of their lords, were refusing to serve unless they were paid excessive wages; while others preferred to beg in idleness rather than work for a living. Edward then ordained that every man and woman in the realm, of whatever condition, free or bondsmen, able-bodied and below sixty years of age, and who were not engaged in commerce or crafts, nor having any land of their own to work, "shall be required to serve in any suitable service, considering his condition, shall be bound to serve him who required him, and shall receive only such wages, allowances, hire or salary as were accustomed to be offered in the place where he is to serve, in the twentieth year of our reign, or in the average of five or six years preceding."

In 1351 Parliament reassembled (having had to postpone its sessions earlier on account of the Black Death and the undesirability of bringing a large number of people together in one place where the infection might spread). In the same year, it gave statutory force to Edward III's policy. It referred to the fact that little heed had been paid by working people to the ordinance of three years before; "if anyone wanted to have them he was obliged to give them whatever they asked, and either to

Because of the shortage of labour, landlords had to hire extra men at busy times like hay-making or harvest

The Peasants' Revolt: Wat Tyler is killed and Richard II faces the rebels at Smithfield

lose his fruit and crops, or satisfy their greed and arrogance." Indeed, the King had levied heavy fines upon abbots, priors, knights and other persons of rank who had hired people at inflated rates of pay, contrary to his 1349 ordinance. The fines were "100 shillings from some, 40 shillings or 20 shillings from others, according as they were able to pay. Moreover he took 20 shillings from each ploughland throughout the kingdom, and notwithstanding this he also took a fifteenth" (tax equal to a fifteenth of the annual value of landholdings). No doubt Edward III was able to replenish his own depleted exchequer in this way, as well as discourage nationwide inflation. Many labourers were arrested for failure to comply with the ruling, though Parliament complained that many of them escaped from prison and went to hide in the woods and forests. The less fortunate ones were forced to pay crippling fines before being set free. Local court records are full of examples of prosecutions. One in Lincolnshire of 1353 has the following: "The jury present that William de Caburn, of Lymberg, ploughman, will not work except as a day labourer or a monthly labourer. And he will not eat salt meat, but only fresh meat, and for this cause he hath departed from the township, for no man dared to hire him in this fashion contrary to the statute."

Writing soon after the passing of the Statute, William Langland wrote in *Piers Plowman* how some peasants refused to be intimidated:

And then would Wastour not work, but wandren about . . .
Labourers, that have no land to live on but their hands,
Deigned not to dine to-day on yesterday's cabbage,
May no penny-ale please them, nor no piece of bacon,
But if it be fresh flesh or fish, fried or baked,
And that hot and hotter still, to keep the chill from their maw
And, but if he be highly hired, else will he chide
And wail the time that ever he was workman born.
And then curseth he the King, and all his Council with him,
That lay down such laws, the labourers to grieve.

Farm labourers threshing wheat

"When Adam delved and Eve span", a contemporary view of John Ball's famous text

Langland showed great sympathy for the poorest peasants, pointing out that unless they could earn higher wages, they would be ruined by the enormous rise in prices which was also taking place, an argument which has a very modern ring about it. He wrote, "The poorest folk are our neighbours, if we look about us – the prisoners in dungeons and the poor in their hovels, overburdened with children, and rack-rented by landlords. For whatever they save by spinning they spend on rent, or on milk and oatmeal to make gruel and fill the bellies of their children who clamour for food. And they themselves are often famished with hunger, and wretched with the miseries of winter – cold, sleepless nights, when they get up to rock the cradle cramped in a corner, and rise before dawn to card and comb the wool, to wash and scrub and mend, and wind yarn and peel rushes for their rushlights. The miseries of these women who dwell in hovels are too pitiful to read, or describe in verse.

"Yet there are many more who suffer like them – men who go hungry and thirsty all day long, and strive their utmost to hide it – ashamed to beg, or tell their neighbours of their need. I've seen enough of the world to know how they suffer, these men who have many children, and no means but their trade to clothe and feed them. For many hands are waiting to grasp the few pence they earn, and while the Friars feast on roast venison, they have bread and thin ale, with perhaps a scrap of cold meat or stale fish. And on Fridays and fast days a farthing's worth of cockles or a few mussels would be a feast for such folk. I tell you, it would be a real charity to help men so burdened, and comfort these cottagers along with the blind and the lame." Langland condemned the greedy landlords who disregarded the peasants:

> God is deaf now-a-days and deigneth not to hear us,
> And prayers have no power the Plague to stay.
> Yet the wretches of this world take no heed of it,
> Nor for dread of death withdraw them from pride,
> Nor share their plenty with the poor;
> But in gaiety, in gluttony they glut themselves with wealth,
> And the more they win, wealth and riches,
> And lord it over lands, the less they part with.

In many ways, the stage seemed to be set for revolt, and many writers of the time expressed the fear that a peasant uprising, such as occasionally arose, might erupt into open and bloody revolt.

From Wycliffe to Ball

Although John Wycliffe had been mainly concerned with reform in religious life, some of his words as we have seen gave rise to anxiety in the government. For Wycliffe, and his "Lollard" followers even more so, were not afraid to take the side of the peasants against their land-owners, religious or secular. As Wycliffe wrote, "Strifes, contests and debates have been used in our land, for lords strive with their tenants to bring them in thraldom more than they should by reason and charity." He added that often lords persecuted their tenants and peasants with unreasonable fines and "amercements". They "despise them, and menace and sometimes beat them when they ask their pay." He accused the lords of devouring poor men's goods with their gluttony, leaving them to perish from hunger and cold, and their children too. "And if their rent be not readily paid their beasts are distressed [seized], and they pursued without mercy."

The embers of revolt were vigorously fanned by one John Ball, a priest who had started to make a name for himself as a popular preacher, "speaking ill of both ecclesiastics and secular lords." The same writer added that he had "rather won the goodwill of the common people than merit in the sight of God." It was said that he taught the people

Richard II, the boy-king, holding a court surrounded by the chief nobles and clergy of England

Rebels, whether against church or state, were dealt with harshly throughout the Middle Ages

not to pay their tithes unless they were better off than the rector or vicar to whom they were due: why should a poor peasant subsidise someone who was better off?

After a time, the authorities caught up with Ball, and he was often thrown into prison. But, as Jean Froissart wrote, Ball only became stronger in his revolutionary talk, collecting crowds around him on Sundays as they came out of church, and addressing them: "My friends, the state of England cannot be right until everything is held communally, and until there is no distinction between nobleman and serf." As Ball put it, "We are all descended from Adam and Eve. How then can they say they are better lords than us, except in making us toil and earn for them to spend?" He accused the nobility of dressing themselves in velvet and furs, leaving the poor to wear cloth; of feasting on wine, spices and good bread while the peasantry had to exist on rye, old straw, and water. "They have fine houses and manors, and we have to brave the wind and the rain as we toil in the fields."

Ball appealed to the common folk to join him in presenting their grievances to the young King, Richard II, who had come to the throne as a boy in 1377. In the summer of 1381 Ball sent messengers and supporters into the towns and villages of southern England to prepare for a march on London. Since all this was treason and sedition, he had to do all this in secret, and his messengers spread the news of the uprising in coded verses like this:

> *John Ball*
> *Greeteth you all,*
> *And doth you to understand*
> *He hath rung your bell.*
> *Now with right and might,*
> *Will and skill,*
> *God speed every dell!*

The immediate cause of the rising which was to be known as the Peasants' Revolt was the government's decision to raise a poll tax, in other words a head tax on every person in the land over the age of fifteen years. Indeed, the government had levied three such taxes between 1377 and 1380, and to many thousands of folk eking out a living on the hard land, this was the second great injustice in a generation, since the Black Death of 1348, with all the hardship in the countryside that this calamity had brought in its wake. In 1381, thousands of people refused to pay the taxes, following the example of those of a forceful temper; and when the government sent out officials to try and enforce collection, by means of juries and informants, the trouble quickly escalated, and the news of revolt in one part of the country quickly inflamed opinion in the neighbouring parts. As the *Chronicon Angliae* tells us, "The peasants, whom we call villeins or bondsmen, with the rural inhabitants in Essex, coveting greater things, and in hopes of reducing everything into subjection to themselves, came together in great multitude, and began to make great tumult, demanding their liberty." Some of their leaders tried to intimidate those who were slow to take up the cry, by threatening to destroy their goods, burn down their houses and cut off their heads. Soon, thousands of people, from Kent, Essex and nearby counties, were marching to London, stopping pilgrims who were wending their way to Canterbury and making them swear to join them as soon as possible. Rochester Castle was stormed; prisons were thrown open and the inmates set free. And John Ball was joined by two other peasant leaders, Wat Tyler and Jack Straw.

After a great deal of fearful deliberation, the Privy Council agreed that the boy-king should meet the peasants and address them in person, appeal to their loyalty, and ask them to disperse after hearing their grievances. In the meantime, on the open fields of Blackheath outside London, John Ball was preaching his famous revolutionary text to the expectant 20,000 rebels who were encamped there:

When Adam delved and Eve span,
Who was then the gentleman?

But after witnessing the size and anger of the waiting crowd, the authorities decided that it would be too dangerous for the young king to meet the rebels face to face. The news of this change of decision provoked a bitter reaction among the common folk. At once they set out to march the remaining few miles into London. They "destroyed on the way a number of houses belonging to lawyers, courtiers and the clergy. . . . Altogether they did great damage in the suburbs, and threatened those who had closed the gates of London Bridge" – the only bridge over the River Thames at that date – "saying that they would burn all the suburbs, take London by force, and burn and destroy everything." At last the rebel army entered London itself, and wrought much damage, destroying the Palace of Savoy belonging to John of Gaunt, murdering Archbishop Simon of Sudbury who as Lord Chancellor had been largely responsible for the poll tax, and ransacking the Temple, the home of the lawyers, where many manorial records were stored. They even got into the Tower of London as the King was coming out, and "four hundred of the mob, led by Tyler, Straw and Ball, dashed in by force and rushed from room to room." It was here that Sudbury was killed. Many Londoners were slaughtered in the streets where they lived and worked by these provincial invaders.

At length there seemed to be no choice but for the King to meet the rebel leaders. This took place at Smithfield, an open space outside the City of London. Wat Tyler soon gave proof of the mood of many of the rebels. "He took the King by the hand, and shook his arm forcibly and roughly, saying to him, 'Brother, be of good comfort and joyful, for you shall have in the fortnight that is to come praise from the commons even more than you have yet, and we shall be good companions!'"

As Richard tried to speak quietly and sensibly to Tyler, the rebel leader's behaviour grew more uncouth and provocative, until a Kentish squire was moved to shout out that he was the "greatest thief and robber in Kent!" Tyler lunged at him with a dagger, and when the Lord Mayor of London tried to grapple with him the dagger was plunged into the Lord Mayor's chest, which luckily was protected with armour beneath the robes. Another knight pushed forward and ran Tyler through two or three times with a sword, and Tyler fell back on the horse where he sat, "crying to the commons to avenge him" – and fell unconscious. There followed a moment of extreme danger, as a troop of archers among the rebels raised their longbows to fire upon the King, but Richard, stepping forward with great personal courage addressed them in a loud voice, "Gentlemen, what do you want? You have no other captain than me. I am your King! Keep the peace!" As an eyewitness recalled, "When they saw and heard the King speak, most of the crowd were quite abashed, and the more peaceful of them began to disperse." The moment of danger was over.

The murder of Simon Sudbury, Archbishop of Canterbury

As the spirit of the rebels in London began to ebb away, rebellions were still in progress in other parts of the country, although the authorities were able to gain the upper hand. In Norwich, Bishop Hugh Despenser gathered together a force of archers and men-at-arms, and took most of the rebels prisoner. "And the Bishop first confessed them, and then beheaded them," saving their souls before despatching their bodies. John Ball was captured and hanged, as were others of the leaders. Fourteenth-century justice began to run its harsh course, at least in the first few months after the revolt, though more leniency was shown in the later stages. As this little contemporary rhyme puts it,

Man beware and be no fool,
Think upon the axe and of the stool!
The stool was hard, the axe was sharp,
The fourth year of King Richard.

In many ways, the institution of serfdom was already in decline before the rising of 1381, in the changed social conditions following the Black Death a generation before. Some landlords still reigned over their villeins like the old-style feudal magnates, but more and more of them were preferring to free their serfs and hire day labourers to work their land. By the time of Chaucer's death in October, 1400, serfdom or villeinage was in many shires a fast-fading relic of an extinct social order.

By the time of the death of Richard II in 1399, at the end of Chaucer's own life, the author of the *Canterbury Tales* had witnessed many great changes in the quality of English life, and the passing of many of the old medieval ways and customs. Then, as now, the older men complained of the fading of the old order, and the unaccustomed prevalence of unwelcome novelties; while the younger, with their new ideas, and their new and outlandish forms of dress, claimed a changing world for themselves.

A Table of Dates

1307	Accession of Edward II
1327	Murder of Edward II at Warwick Castle: accession of Edward III
1332	Probable year of birth of William Langland, author of *Piers Plowman*
1338	Opening of the Hundred Years' War with France
1340	The Battle of Sluys; approximate birth date of Geoffrey Chaucer
1344–48	Founding of the Order of the Garter
1346	The Battle of Crécy, victory of the English over the French
1348	The Black Death reaches England: a third of the population perish within a year
1351	The Statute of Labourers: the government seeks to limit wages to the level existing before the Black Death and the ensuing inflation
1356	The Battle of Poitiers
1362	First version of *Piers Plowman* by William Langland
1374	Chaucer becomes Controller of Wine Customs in the Port of London
1376	Death of the Black Prince
1377	Death of Edward III
	Accession of Richard II
1381	The Peasants' Revolt; death of Wat Tyler and John Ball
1384	Death of John Wycliffe
1389	Chaucer appointed Clerk of the King's Works
1399	Death of John of Gaunt
	Deposition of Richard II: accession of Henry IV
1400	Death of Geoffrey Chaucer
1415	Battle of Agincourt
1431	Burning of Joan of Arc as a heretic
1453	End of the Hundred Years' War

A Medieval Glossary

ALCHEMY Medieval term for chemistry and in particular the search for a way of changing base metals into gold.

APOTHECARY Druggist or maker of medicines.

APPRENTICE Young man indentured to the master of a trade or craft for a period of seven years.

BAILIFF A manorial official responsible for supervising the workers on the land.

BUTTERY Place in a manor house or other household for storing wines and ales under the supervision of a butler or "bottler".

CHAPERON Form of medieval hood or cloak.

CHIVALRY High code of conduct to which medieval knights aspired or at least paid lip service.

CONYE Rabbit.

COTTE A tunic worn by ordinary medieval folk.

DESMESNE That part of an estate that the lord farmed himself, instead of letting out to tenants.

FRANCHISE A "freedom" or area in which the King's writ did not apply.

FRIAR Priests who travelled around the country to preach the gospel.

HAUBERK A knight's coat of mail.

HEAUME The heavy steel helmet of a knight.

HUMOURS The fluids of the body thought to determine human character, namely blood, phlegm, choler, melancholy.

JOURNEYMAN Craftsman or tradesman employed by the day.

JOUST A form of tournament in which two knights charged each other on horseback with lances.

LOLLARD Follower of John Wycliffe.

MACHICOLATION Castle parapet fitted with openings through which missiles could be dropped on attackers below.

MANCIPLE Official in a medieval household responsible for catering.

MARCHES The border lands between England and Wales.

MASTERPIECE Work performed by an apprentice at the completion of his apprenticeship by which his master judged his skill.

MAZER Toasting bowl made of maple wood.

MELANCHOLIC A tendency towards sadness and depression determined by the humours of the body.

MÊLÉE A form of tournament fought between two opposing bands of knights.

NEF Ornate salt cellar in the shape of a ship.

PAGE The son of a nobleman or gentleman undertaking service in a noble household as a training in social and martial skills.

PARDONER Medieval priest or cleric who made a living, often fraudulently, by selling Papal indulgences.

PELISSE   Woman's mantle with arm holes or sleeves which reached down to the ankles.

PLURALISM   The practice by which a priest held more than one living simultaneously.

QUINTAIN   A moving shield attached to a wooden post used in jousting practice.

REEVE   A magistrate or county official. The word "sheriff" is derived from "Shire-reeve".

ROOD   The cross of Christ or crucifix.

SANGUINE   The temperament of a person in which blood predominates over the other humours.

SCUTAGE   Literally, shield money: money paid by feudal landowners in lieu of personal military service.

SIMONY   The practice of buying or selling preferment in the Church.

SQUIRE   A young nobleman or son of a gentleman who had graduated from the status of page and aspired to the status of knighthood.

STEWARD   The household official responsible for accounts.

TOLL BOOTH   Place in a town hall where disputes concerning markets and fairs were settled.

TOURNAMENT   Mock battle fought between knights or groups of knights on horseback or on foot.

TRENCHER   Dinner plate.

WAIT   Band of musicians maintained by a city or town, e.g. to sing carols at Christmas.

WASSAIL   Festive occasion or drinking bout.

VILLEIN   Peasant or serf who held a small strip of land in return for rendering menial service to his lord.

VIZOR   The hinged face guard on a helmet which contained eye-slits.

YEOMAN   Term applied to the independent tenant farmer.

The Medieval Cost of Living

It is difficult to make comparisons between the cost of living in Chaucer's day, and in our own time. Society was organised very differently: many of the poorest peasants, with an income of only £2 or £3 a year nevertheless managed to get by with a certain amount of home produce, and pickings and gleanings when they brought in the harvest or rendered other services to their lord as part of their tenancy. But the following examples of prices and incomes in Chaucer's day will certainly show the spread of wealth from the richest earl to the poorest villein. For the most part the rich escaped taxation, but the poor did not; it was they who bore the burden of church tithes or "tenths" of their income, and who found it hardest to pay the occasional poll taxes levied on each member of the population regardless of rank or wealth. The sums quoted below are the actual amounts which existed when Chaucer was alive. Now that we have adopted decimal currency, it might be worth a reminder that 12 pence made one shilling, and 20 shillings one pound. £1 approximately equals $2.50 today, and one penny roughly one cent. The best modern account of the subject is to be found in John Burnett's *History of the Cost of Living* published as a Pelican paperback.

Prices

Price of a gallon of Bordeaux wine from a wine merchant: threepence to fivepence a gallon.

Cost of ploughing land three times, sixpence an acre.

Cost of hoeing, a penny an acre.

Cost of reaping, fivepence an acre.

Cost of marling (fertilizing) the soil, three to eight shillings an acre.

Average value of a villein's estate, £5.

Average value of a villein's household goods, £2.

Amount spent on bread each year by an average peasant family, about £1.

Price of a pair of leather boots, two shillings.

Price of bricks for building, about eighteen pence per 1,000.

Price of a gallon of barley ale, about a halfpenny.

Annual basic budget of a student at Oxford or Cambridge University, about £3.

Writing paper (parchment) cost about ten shillings for 240 sheets.

An Oxford student found guilty of using a threatening weapon could be fined four shillings, and more than six shillings for an actual assault.

Cost of a good horse, from £30 upward.

Cost of a falcon, from £5 upward.

Cost of a good war horse, between £40 and £80.

Price of the cheapest blanket or russet material for peasant clothing, a shilling a yard.

Price of a rich scarlet gown trimmed with fur, about £20.

A sack of raw wool cost from £3 to £13, according to quality.

Price of a cheap robe as worn by a clerk at a nobleman's court, about £2.

Price of a cheap pair of shoes, about sixpence.

Fine for depositing garbage in the streets, imposed at the time of the Black Death, forty pence for the first offence, and six shillings and eightpence for each subsequent offence.

Cost of a fat ox after the Black Death, four shillings.

Cost of a cow after the Black Death, twelve pence.

Cost of a heifer after the Black Death, sixpence.

Cost of a lamb after the Black Death, twopence.

Cost of a large pig after the Black Death, fivepence.

Incomes

Income from 20 acres of land, about £4 per annum rent.

Wage of a hired labourer on the land, or an artisan in the towns, about £2 to £3 a year.

Daily wage of a thatcher's assistant, about a penny before the Black Death and twopence or threepence a day in later years.

Daily wage of a master mason or carpenter working on a great cathedral, up to about tenpence a day.

Daily wage of an ordinary carpenter or sawyer, about fourpence a day.

Annual income of Richard, Earl of Cornwall and brother of Henry III, about £5,000 (untaxed).

Annual income of poorer members of the nobility, about £1,000 (untaxed).

With the revenue from their Church lands, the bishops were often as wealthy as some of the nobility.

Daily wage of a lord's huntsman seven or eight pence a day.

Daily wage of a fowler (hunting attendant), about the same.

Daily wage of the Prince of Wales as a soldier, 20 shillings.

Daily wage of an earl in battle, six shillings and eightpence.

Daily wage of a baron in battle, four shillings.

Daily wage of a knight in battle, two shillings.

Daily wage of an archer in battle, threepence.

Daily wage of a spearman and infantryman, twopence.

Stipend of a chaplain before the Black Death, about £5 and £10 after.

Stipend of a priest before the Black Death, about £10, and £20 after.

Pay of Justices of the Peace when at Quarter Sessions, four shillings a day.

Pay of the Clerk to the Justices at Quarter Sessions, two shillings a day.

Further Reading

The Fourteenth Century, May McKisack (Oxford University Press, London, 1959; Oxford University Press, New York, 1959).

Historical Interpretation: Sources of Medieval History, J. J. Bagley (Pelican Books, London, 1965; Penguin Books, Baltimore, 1965).

Making of the English Landscape, W. G. Hoskins (Pelican Books, London, 1965)

Life on the English Manor, H. S. Bennett (Oxford University Press, London, 1969; Oxford University Press, New York, 1965).

The Later Middle Ages, George Holmes (Nelson, London, 1969; Thomas Nelson, Camden, New Jersey, 1962).

Medicine in Medieval England, C. H. Talbot (Oldbourne, London, 1967).

English Warfaring Life in The Middle Ages, J. J. Jusserand (Benn, London, 1950; Saunders, Philadelphia, 1950).

A Short History of English Agriculture, W. H. R. Curtler (Oxford University Press, London, 1909).

Illustrated English Social History: Chaucer's England and The Early Tudors, G. Trevelyan (Longmans, London, 1954).

Pharmacy in History, G. E. Trease (Balliere, Tindall & Cassell, London, 1964; Williams & Wilkins, Baltimore, 1965).

History of Everyday Things in England, Marjorie & C. H. B. Quennell (Batsford, London, 1968; Putnam, New York, 1971).

A History of London Life, R. J. Mitchell & M. D. R. Leys (Longman, London 1958; Penguin, Baltimore, 1963).

Medieval Warfare, Geoffrey Hindley (Wayland, London, 1971; Putnam, New York, 1971).

Chaucer's World, Maurice Hussey (Cambridge University Press, New York, 1967).

Canterbury Tales, Geoffrey Chaucer (Penguin, London 1953; Penguin, Baltimore, 1953).

Piers Plowman, William Langland (Penguin, London, 1953; John Hopkins, Baltimore, 1971.

The Black Death, Philip Ziegler (Collins, London, 1969; John Day, New York, 1969).

Picture Credits

Index